A GUIDE TO
SOCIOLOGICAL
THINKING

A GUIDE TO

SOCIOLOGICAL

THINKING

VINCENT RYAN RUGGIERO

SAGE Publications
International Educational and Professional Publisher
Thousand Oaks   London   New Delhi

HM
45
.R84
1996

For information address:

SAGE Publications, Inc.
2455 Teller Road
Thousand Oaks, California 91320
E-mail: order@sagepub.com

SAGE Publications Ltd.
6 Bonhill Street
London EC2A 4PU
United Kingdom

SAGE Publications India Pvt. Ltd.
M-32 Market
Greater Kailash I
New Delhi 110 048 India

Printed in the United States of America

Library of Congress Cataloging-in-Publication Data

Ruggiero, Vincent Ryan.
   A guide to sociological thinking / Vincent Ryan Ruggiero.
      p. cm.
   Includes bibliographical references and index.
   ISBN 0-8039-5741-6 (cloth: alk. paper). — ISBN 0-8039-5742-4
(pbk.: alk. paper)
      1. Sociology—Study and teaching. 2. Critical thinking.
   3. Thought and thinking. I. Title.
   HM45.R84 1995
   302—dc20   95-39046

This book is printed on acid-free paper.

96 97 98 99 10 9 8 7 6 5 4 3 2 1

Sage Production Editor: Astrid Virding
Sage Copy Editor: Joyce Kuhn
Sage Typesetter: Janelle LeMaster

Contents

Introduction

Throughout this century numerous educational philosophers have urged that teaching not be limited to presenting students with information to remember and recall. Whatever is learned that way, they have pointed out, is all too quickly forgotten and the teacher must devote an inordinate amount of time to reviewing what was presented in previous semesters. In contrast, when students engage a course intellectually, grapple with the same issue that practitioners of the discipline encounter, and develop strategies for generating and evaluating ideas, their learning is likely to be both deep and lasting.

Stanford's Lee Shulman classifies knowledge in three broad categories: propositions (factual information), actual cases in the particular discipline, and procedures (cognitive strategies). Most modern textbooks in sociology, like those in other disciplines, do an excellent job with propositional knowledge; some also do a very good job with case knowledge. Unfortunately, few do much, if anything, with the central component of cognitive learning: procedural knowledge.

This book is designed to increase sociology students' cognitive learning. It draws on the insights of a number of educational reform initiatives, including **critical, creative,** and **reflective** thinking, active learning, and problem-based education. Its objectives are as follows:

- To build appreciation of the intellectual environment and adventure of sociological inquiry and of the relevance of that inquiry to students' lives
- To develop understanding of the three stages of the thinking process—reflective, creative, and critical
- To develop skill in applying the thinking process to sociological issues
- To promote the habits and attitudes associated with excellence in thinking
- To encourage students to enter the discipline's ongoing dialogue

This book is an ancillary text, so it does not present the field of sociology as an introductory sociology text would. All decisions about chapter division, structure, and content have been made in light of the book's purpose—to help students learn to think more deeply and effectively about sociology. Most examples used in the book are micro- rather than macrosociological because these tend to be closer to students' experience.

1

❦

The Role of
Thinking in Sociology

Contrary to popular misconception, sociology is neither a kind of social work nor a collection of commonsense notions about society. It is the scientific study of collective human behavior, and its focus is broader than most other disciplines, in particular the other social sciences. Biology focuses on the physical nature of animal and plant life, psychology on human behavior, and anthropology on the origin and development of human beings and their societies. But sociology is concerned with the interplay between people's purposive behavior, which sociologists call human agency, and the various social organizations—home, school, church, government, business, the entertainment and communication media, and so on.

If you've bought into the popular stereotype of scientific research, you may expect sociology to be boring stuff—a collection of dry, lifeless data without much relevance to everyday life, assembled by boring people whose idea of excitement is swapping statistical correlations. If that is your dread, you're in for a pleasant surprise. The questions that interest sociologists include the following:

- What prompted the crowds to line the Los Angeles freeway and cheer O. J. Simpson as he drove by holding a gun to his head?
- Which occupations are most respected, and why?
- Can membership in fraternities and sororities influence people's eating patterns?
- Do males who work in traditionally female occupations face any special difficulties?
- What lessons about gender, if any, are learned in school?
- Do people tend to be less helpful and friendly at night than in the daytime?

As these questions suggest, sociologists' curiosity is focused on matters of wide and general interest, sometimes on the same subjects covered in the supermarket tabloids. Unlike the tabloids, of course, sociology is neither titillating nor glitzy; its focus is reality rather than fantasy. Nevertheless, the exchange of ideas it sparks is vigorous, often passionate, and both intellectually challenging and rewarding.

Throughout the ages, philosophers speculated about society and social behavior but without attempting to validate their theories through scientific methods. The use of such methods distinguishes sociology from social philosophy. Sociology began in the 19th century, the product of the social change wrought by the Industrial Revolution and the development of the natural sciences. At that time, three famous individuals all asked the question "How does society evolve?" and each gave a different answer. French philosopher Auguste Comte (1798-1857), who invented the term "sociology," believed that all societies go through three stages—religious, metaphysical, and scientific—and that the sociologist's role is to guide society's evolution. English philosopher Herbert Spencer (1820-1903) claimed that society evolves through the Darwinian process of natural selection, the "survival of the fittest," and therefore no human guidance is necessary. German-born Karl Marx (1818-1883), rejecting both Comte's and Spencer's views, argued that economic exploitation breeds class conflict, which becomes the catalyst of change.

Although all three extolled the application of scientific method to the study of society, none of them engaged in scientific observation or experimentation. French sociologist Emile Durkheim (1858-1917), who pioneered in classifying sociology as a social *science*, codified his approach in *The Rules of Sociological Method* (1895). Durkheim contended that sociologists should focus exclusively on what can be observed and measured; thus he argued that people's subjective experiences, beliefs, and interpretations were not a proper matter for sociological research or theorizing. His famous German contemporary, Max Weber (1864-1920), disputed that view, arguing that the link between human behavior, on the one hand, and human perception and thought, on the other, is too strong to be ignored, that scientific observation is meaningful only when it occurs in a context of sympathetic understanding of people's thought processes and values.

By 1900, sociological emphasis in the United States had become less theoretical and more practical than its European counterpart, more directed at applying knowledge to solve specific social problems. Disagreements between theoreticians and pragmatists and between objectivists and subjectivists have arisen from time to time throughout this century, but today (perhaps temporarily), the consensus favors a balance between competing views. One prominent contemporary disagreement concerns the issue of social dynamics, that is, what specific forces are most influential in society and how they exert their influence. *Functionalists* contend that the various agencies of society (family, school, and so on) achieve stability by building consensus. *Symbolic interactionists* see individual interpretation and interaction as more significant than the cooperation of agencies. *Conflict theorists* argue that conflict is the central focus of social life and the catalyst for change. (For Marxists and neo-Marxists, the specific conflict is class struggle.) *Feminists* contend that the most fundamental social reality has been the dominance of men over women and that the greatest imperative is to redress womens' grievances. These differences of viewpoint are manifested not only in formal debate but also in research decisions.

Far from being the dusty collection of data projected by the stereotype, sociology retains its vitality by being responsive to changing social conditions. During the 1960s, the rebellion of American youth prompted a shift in sociological research from the socialization of children to parent-youth relationships; over the next two decades, as the percentage of elderly people increased, researchers became interested in the relationships between adults and their parents. The increase in the number of married women in the workplace has raised issues of child care and equity in the performance of household tasks. Similarly, as the divorce and remarriage rates have risen over the past 50 years, new social problems have commanded attention—for example, economic complications attending divorce settlements and tension between children and stepparents as well as among stepsiblings.

New research findings are published regularly, and so existing sociological interpretations, theories, concepts, and approaches are continually being tested. A notable example of the impact that new theories can have on the field is the advent of the feminist perspective in sociology. Central to that view is the claim that sociological research (and that in other fields) traditionally ignored or trivialized the role of women in history and the impact of gender discrimination in socialization, education, and employment. This charge has provoked a lively, continuing (and sometimes heated) debate, prompted a reexamination of the entire body of sociological literature, and widened the focus of research.

At this very moment someone is likely to be identifying an inconsistency or contradiction that had gone unnoticed, or applying existing knowledge in a new and exciting way, or discovering that an older view, previously dismissed as archaic, contains an essential insight lacking in contemporary theory and practice. You are welcome to join the ongoing dialogue even if you are only a beginning student of sociology—provided you meet a few minimal requirements:

- First, you should be curious about issues and willing to invest the time and effort necessary to find the most accurate and complete answers to your questions.
- Second, you should already have or be willing to adopt the habit of evaluating ideas on the basis of evidence rather than on the basis of whether they agree with your prior opinions or the current intellectual fashion.
- Finally, you should be aware of the limitations of your knowledge and willingness to learn from others. That doesn't mean you must accept everything you read or hear. On the contrary, the aim of this book is to help you think independently, as all good sociologists do, selecting worthy issues for analysis, asking penetrating questions, consulting available research (in some cases conducting your own research), reaching sound conclusions, and presenting your ideas persuasively.

These requirements may seem too obvious and elementary to need stating, but for several decades popular culture has promoted contrary notions, and many people seem to have been influenced by this message. (The most common of these notions will be the focus of discussions in various sections of this book.)

Common Issues in Sociology

As I have noted, sociology is not a collection of facts to be memorized but an ongoing inquiry into matters of social importance. Controversies arise in sociology, as in other fields, largely because each of the various research areas can be viewed from many different perspectives and interests. Many sociologists of education, for instance, focus on the content of classroom instruction and its relationship to social values and belief systems. Others are interested in teaching methods and their relative effectiveness in achieving desired outcomes. Additional matters of emphasis are administrative structures and their impact on faculty morale, assessment of student performance, the impact of technology on learning, comparison of institutional efficiency within and among the states, and the developing phenomenon of business-school and media-school partnerships.

Although no two issues are precisely alike in their particulars, the broad classifications of controversy are relatively few in number. By recognizing them, you can achieve deeper understanding in your reading and listening and clearer focus in your own analyses. Here are the main classifications, together with relevant questions:

- Issues of fact. In this most fundamental of issues, the important questions are "What really happened in the incident (the actual sequence of events and the people involved in them)?"; "Did the authority really hold the view that is attributed to him or her?"; and "Were the data completely and correctly reported?"

- Issues of interpretation. Here the concern centers not on the facts but on the way they are understood. The essential question is "What interpretation is most reasonable?"

- Issues of cause. The focus of these issues in on *why* something happened. The principal question to be asked is "What action or condition created or influenced this situation?"

- Issues of responsibility. These issues are related to those of cause, except that they concern not the events themselves but accountability for them. The essential question is "Who was (were) in control of the situation and therefore, arguably, culpable for it?"

- Issues of effect. Here the disagreement is over the consequences of an event or phenomenon. Where the consequences have already occurred, the main question is "Are these effects attributable to the prior event or phenomenon?" Where the consequences have not occurred, the question is "What are the effects likely to be?"

- Ethical issues. Such issues address whether behavior is morally right or wrong. The principal question to be asked is "Does the behavior in question violate any moral obligation or ideal?" (Examples: the obligation to keep a professional confidence or honor an acknowledged commitment; the ideal of justice, fairness, or honesty.) Sociologists address moral issues in either of two ways: considering whether the phenomena under study have moral implications and designing and carrying out their own research activities.

- Issues of effectiveness or efficiency. These issues concern whether a plan of action will accomplish the intended objective at all or whether it will do so at a reasonable cost of time, energy, and/or money. The key question here is "How strong is the evidence that this plan will work (or work efficiently)?"

- Issues of priority. Typically in this type of issue, people agree that two competing points of view or courses of action are meritorious but disagree over which is the more important. The question to be addressed is "Which point of view or course of action takes precedence and why?"

Few if any sociological conclusions have received unanimous endorsement. Pitirim A. Sorokin (1927) challenged the established notion that education decreases intellectual and social differences in society, writing as follows:

Contrary to the common opinion, universal education . . . leads not so much to an obliteration of mental and social differences as to their increase. The school, even the most democratic school, open to everybody, if it performs its task properly, is a machinery of the "aristocratization" and stratification of society, not of "leveling" and "democratization." (pp. 189-190)

More recently, G. William Domhoff (1995) has argued that "there is a ruling social class in the United States" consisting of "the owners and managers of large corporations" (p. 217). According to Domhoff, although these individuals represent only about 1% of the population, they hold more than a quarter of all private wealth and two thirds of privately held corporate wealth. Moreover, they "receive 20 to 25 percent of the yearly income, direct the large corporations and foundations, and dominate the federal government in Washington" (p. 218). Domhoff believes that this cohesive social network exerts significant influence on social politics and the climate of public opinion. According to Domhoff, however, "Most social scientists disagree with this view" (p. 218).

A dispute continues about why religious fundamentalism has grown in America. Some sociologists attribute the change to higher fertility rates among fundamentalists than among other groups (e.g., Bibby & Brinkerhoff, 1973). Others argue that many Christians embraced fundamentalism when liberal denominations turned from traditional spiritual concerns to social activism. Still others maintain that many moderate religious believers have grown more conservative, and more vocal, mainly in response to the influence of secularism in government, education, and the entertainment media.

The long-accepted view of prehistoric society has been challenged by a new theory. Traditionally, sociologists believed that males made the most important contribution to prehistoric society by hunting and gathering while women stayed in the cave and cared for children. The new theory hypothesizes that women made an equal contribution by fashioning tools for digging, storing food, and carrying infants (see Giele, 1988, p. 312).

Even some of the most fundamental issues sociologists inherited from social philosophers, issues debated since the time of ancient Greece, are often contested. Especially noteworthy is the nurture versus nature issue, the essential question being whether environmental influences such as socialization or genetic constitution exert the greatest influence on human thought, feeling, and action. It is a question of the greatest significance because it has implications for law, education, and government as well as for the various sciences, social sciences, and humanities.

The Thinking Process

Knowing what one is thinking about is as important as the proverbial knowing what one is talking about. Even accomplished thinkers would be hard pressed to draw insights from ignorance or misunderstanding. Accurate reading, listening, and observing are therefore essential to the success of the thinking process even though they are not themselves a part of that process. In the discussion of thinking that follows in this and subsequent chapters, the prior importance of accurate comprehension should be understood.

The term "thinking process," as it is used in this book, refers to the combination of intellectual activities employed in identifying and resolving issues. This process has three stages—reflective, creative, and critical—each of which has certain defining characteristics, habits, and skills that can be mastered through practice. Some of these characteristics are common to all three, most notably asking questions, although, as subsequent chapters will demonstrate, the focus of the questions differs among the stages.

THE THREE STAGES OF THINKING

Reflective

This phase consists of equal parts observation and wonder. The most effective sociologists not only deal skillfully with challenges that have already been identified; they are also proficient at *identifying* challenges. In other words, they continually look for areas in which the field's perspective needs broadening or deepening, reconsider old perspectives, speculate about new possibilities (or old ones unwisely abandoned), and approach old ideas in a new way.

Unlike the other kinds of thinking, reflective thinking is private and therefore seldom shared with others. Its emphasis is *exploration:* finding interesting and promising issues for analysis. Because this kind of thinking makes no claim, takes no stand, expresses no viewpoint other than "this seems a worthy matter to examine," it carries no danger of being wrong, no risk of losing face. Nothing is off-limits to reflective thinking—every theory, concept, perspective, and method is open to question.

Creative

This is the stage at which ideas are produced. Mastery of this process opens the mind to insight and increases the chance that the response will be original, but it does not guarantee an original response to every challenge. Nor does it imply that innovative ideas are necessarily better than established ones. The fundamental test of any idea is how effectively it solves the problem or resolves the issue in question. A response that fails this test is unacceptable, no matter how imaginative and unique it might otherwise be; conversely, a response that passes this test is acceptable, whether or not it is original. Only on those occasions when the creative thinking process succeeds in producing an idea that is both uncommonly good and uncommon is that *idea* termed creative. (Finding an innovative way of expressing an established idea would, of course, count as creative *expression*.) The ideas generated may take any of a number of forms, including procedures, formulas, principles, concepts, and theories.

Myths about creativity are abundant, so it is important to know the facts. First, creativity is not confined to the arts. A sculptor, painter, or musician may be creative but so may an engineer, an architect, a scientist, a sales clerk, or a sociologist. Virtually any challenge can be approached more, or less, creatively. Second, almost anyone can learn to be imaginative, ingenious, and insightful. Third, drugs (including alcohol) diminish rather than enhance creative achievement. Although in recent decades it has been fashionable to believe that drugs stimulate the creative process, the evidence has never supported that idea. Like any other intellectual activity, creativity demands clearheadedness, concentration, and discipline; drugs produce the opposite effects.

Finally, creativity is associated with mental health. Although an occasional researcher may claim that mental illness promotes creativity, most researchers, including Erich Fromm, Rollo May, Carl Rogers, Abraham Maslow, J. P. Guilford, and Ernest Hilgard, reject this notion:

The consensus of these authors is that creativity is an expression of a mentally or psychologically healthy person, that creativity is associated with wholeness, unity, honesty, integrity, personal involvement, enthusiasm, high motivation, and action.

There is also agreement that neurosis either accompanies or causes a degraded quality of one's creativity. For neurotic persons and persons with other forms of mental disease (who are, at the same time, creative) such assumptions as the following are offered: that these persons are creative in spite of their disease; that they are producing below the achievements they would show without the disease; that they are on the downgrade, or that they are pseudo creative, that is, they may have brilliant original ideas which, because of the neurosis, they do not communicate. (Anderson, 1959, p. 258)

Critical

This is the stage at which ideas are evaluated. When applied to your own thinking, it *follows* reflective and creative thinking, appraising the ideas you have generated and correcting any errors you may have committed. When applied to other people's ideas, which presumably were generated out of *their* reflective and creative thinking, critical thinking is used independently of the other kinds of thinking. Critical thinking serves to reveal to what extent an idea or argument fits the evidence and meets the requirement of logic. The ability to think critically, like the ability to think creatively, is not inborn but learned; although individuals undoubtedly differ in their native capacity for such thinking, virtually everyone can master the fundamentals.

PATTERNS OF THINKING

Although these three stages of the thinking process are, broadly speaking, sequential, that sequence is sometimes interrupted or repeated. Figure 1.1 illustrates some common thinking patterns, with the stages indicated parenthetically.

Simple Sequence	Interrupted Sequence
PONDERING a reading, listening, or observing experience; asking probing questions about it; identifying an issue to be resolved (**reflective**) ▼ PRODUCING possible answers to the questions and diverse views on the issue, with supportive arguments and evidence (**creative**) ▼ EVALUATING the ideas produced and deciding which view is most in keeping with the evidence (**critical**)	PONDERING a reading, listening, or observing experience; asking probing questions about it; identifying an issue to be resolved (**reflective**) ▼ PRODUCING possible answers to the questions and diverse views on the issue, with supportive arguments and evidence (**creative**) ▼ PONDERING one of the arguments or an item of evidence; identifying a new issue, not directly related to the first, to be resolved later (**reflective**) ▼ RETURNING to the original issue, evaluating the ideas produced and deciding which view is most in keeping with the evidence (**critical**)

Figure 1.1

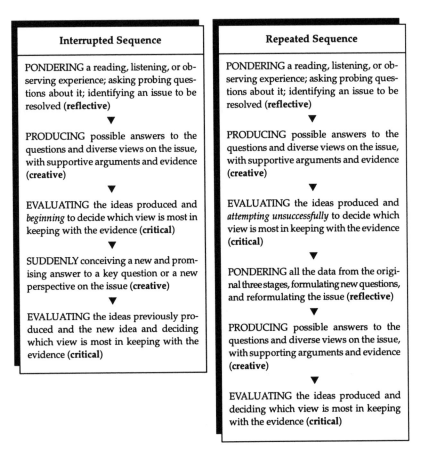

Interrupted Sequence	Repeated Sequence
PONDERING a reading, listening, or observing experience; asking probing questions about it; identifying an issue to be resolved (**reflective**)	PONDERING a reading, listening, or observing experience; asking probing questions about it; identifying an issue to be resolved (**reflective**)
▼	▼
PRODUCING possible answers to the questions and diverse views on the issue, with supportive arguments and evidence (**creative**)	PRODUCING possible answers to the questions and diverse views on the issue, with supportive arguments and evidence (**creative**)
▼	▼
EVALUATING the ideas produced and *beginning* to decide which view is most in keeping with the evidence (**critical**)	EVALUATING the ideas produced and *attempting unsuccessfully* to decide which view is most in keeping with the evidence (**critical**)
▼	▼
SUDDENLY conceiving a new and promising answer to a key question or a new perspective on the issue (**creative**)	PONDERING all the data from the original three stages, formulating new questions, and reformulating the issue (**reflective**)
▼	▼
EVALUATING the ideas previously produced and the new idea and deciding which view is most in keeping with the evidence (**critical**)	PRODUCING possible answers to the questions and diverse views on the issue, with supporting arguments and evidence (**creative**)
	▼
	EVALUATING the ideas produced and deciding which view is most in keeping with the evidence (**critical**)

Figure 1.1 continued

Because traditional intelligence tests do not measure the thinking process, there is no correlation between a person's IQ score and thinking skill. This does not mean that thinking is unimportant; it merely reflects the fact that the IQ test has been misunderstood and applied in ways against which its originator, Alfred Binet, warned. Most researchers on intelligence agree that the concept of intelligence is closely linked to thinking ability.

Howard Gardner, a leading cognitive theorist, suggests that rather than a single kind of intelligence there are actually seven—linguistic, musical, logical-mathematical, spatial, bodily-kinesthetic, interpersonal, and intrapersonal. (In recent years, he has speculated on the possibility of four more—spiritual, humorous, naturalist, and financial.) All have in common the ability to solve problems or produce something.

Thinking and Learning

So far, this chapter has defined important cognitive terms and clarified the importance of thinking in the field of sociology. Now, a very different but equally important question is considered—how you can use your mind in learning a subject, precisely what you can do, and when and how you can do it. The main activities of traditional learning are to read textbooks, listen to professors' lectures, and be prepared to demonstrate understanding of the course material in class discussions and on examinations. In such learning, the emphasis is on *acquiring important information.* Another dimension of learning, often neglected, is *applying your thinking skills to the course materials.* This vital dimension will deepen understanding and assist you in mastering the strategies of sociologists. By including this dimension in your course, your instructor is not only enriching your educational experience but also demonstrating faith in your capacity for higher-order thinking.

The first phase of a thinking approach to reading assignments is identical to that of the traditional approach—**to understand the author's purpose in writing and the content of his or her message.** The readings you are assigned in any sociology course will be informative or persuasive or a combination of the two. Typically, a textbook chapter is written to inform you of some important aspect of the discipline; it may, for example, trace the historical development of the field, discuss a particular social institution such as the family, or introduce you to several important theorists and compare their ideas. An essay, on the other hand, may challenge the prevailing view of a sociological phenomenon—say, racial quotas in business—and advance an argument for a different view. It is not uncommon for this kind of essay to present information in support of the argument, in which case, then, its main aim is to be persuasive and its secondary aim is to be informative.

The essential message of nonfiction prose writing is called the central idea and is expressed early in the piece, often immediately after the introduction, and reinforced (although usually not restated) at the end. All other parts of the writing serve to support and elaborate the central idea. Common techniques in informative writing include explaining factual data, citing examples, narrating historical events, making analogies, describing, detailing a process, defining, quoting, and paraphrasing. Persuasive strategies include many of the preceding as well as classifying, comparing, interpreting, and analyzing.

A widely accepted initial reading strategy is to skim the chapter or essay, identifying the introduction, the central idea, the major headings, and the conclusion. This approach will give you a clear sense of both content and structure even before you begin reading and enable you to read more quickly and efficiently. After skimming, read the piece carefully for the sole purpose of understanding it. Do not pause to underline or make notes; similarly, do not evaluate the message, decide whether you agree or disagree, or ponder how you might respond. (If you mix evaluation with understanding, you may end up doing neither very well.)

The second phase of a thinking approach to reading assignments is **to decide whether to accept all of what you read, part of what you read, or none of what you read.** This may sound like a presumptuous overstepping of your role as a student. Your past experience may have taught you, directly or by implication, that to question a textbook author's or the professor's view is always offensive. That is not the case. (Of course, it *can* be offensive if it is done at the wrong time, in the wrong way, or in the wrong spirit. Chapter 6, "Conducting Sociological Dialogue," explains how to avoid these mistakes.)

Several hundred years ago, Francis Bacon, the British philosopher and essayist, stressed that the purpose of reading (or listening) is not to accept uncritically or to reject arbitrarily but to "weigh and consider." To accomplish this objective, skim the piece of writing a second time immediately after you have completed reading it. Mark the parts that contain important information or deserve careful consideration either because their significance may extend beyond the context of the work or because they raise questions in your mind. Here are some questions that critical readers often ask:

- Where does the author engage in interpretation and/or judgment, as opposed to the simple presentation of factual information? If so, which interpretations and judgments, if any, might reasonably be challenged?
- Does the author reveal a bias for or against any idea or perspective mentioned in the work? If so, does the author seem to control that bias and demonstrate fairmindedness? How would someone who holds an opposing view respond to this question?
- Does the author omit any important consideration? (If you are not well grounded in the subject, this question will be difficult to answer, but you should still be able to spot obvious omissions, such as the failure to mention one entire side of an issue.)
- Do any of the author's conclusions seem to be less than adequately supported by the evidence presented? What other evidence is neces-

sary to support the conclusions? How representative are the cases the author presents?

- Does what you read challenge any of your own opinions or those of people whose views you respect? If so, in what way? (Remember that in cases where you are mistaken, the view that challenges your opinion will be the *correct* view.)

- What questions does this reading raise but not satisfactorily answer? (The fact that such questions exist does not necessarily indicate a deficiency in the author's treatment of the issue. The questions that occur to you may be outside the scope of the article or chapter.)

Answering such questions often demands consulting other sources and comparing their views with those expressed in your reading assignment. (Chapter 4, "Thinking Creatively," discusses basic research sources and strategies.) The fact that sociology has a larger perspective than many other disciplines suggests that sociologists have an unusual opportunity to incorporate other scholars' insights into their thinking. But you will realize this opportunity only if you are willing to cast your investigative net wide—in other words, to read whatever is relevant to the issue, regardless of whether it was written by a sociologist, a biologist, a psychologist, or a philosopher. It is also a sound practice to sample magazines and journals from a variety of perspectives—for a political issue, for example, consult liberal, moderate, and conservative publications. If you aren't sure what the editorial stance of a magazine or journal is, consult the current edition of Bill Katz and Linda Sternberg Katz's *Magazines for Libraries* (published by R. R. Bowker). This volume is a standard reference work available in most libraries. As you read relevant magazine and journal articles, note whether they corroborate or challenge the original author's view.

The next chapter discusses the characteristics associated with excellence in thinking. Subsequent chapters present techniques for thinking reflectively, creatively, and critically, and for presenting your ideas persuasively in writing and in discussion.

INQUIRY

Save your response to the following inquiry. You will need to refer back to it to complete a future assignment.

- ■ Make a list of questions about sociology that occurred to you while reading this chapter. (If none come readily to mind, look back over the chapter.) Add to your list any other matters about society that you have wondered about or engaged in discussions about—questions, for example, about family life, school, religion, politics, movies, music, or television.

2

๒

Characteristics of
Effective Thinkers

No one, no matter how great his or her expertise, has ever achieved perfection in thinking, nor is anyone ever likely to. Respected authors, erudite scholars, and even Nobel laureates make errors from time to time because imperfection is a defining characteristic of humanity. The finest thinkers, in fact, would be the first to acknowledge their fallibility. This is not to say they are satisfied with their vulnerability to error. On the contrary, they are more dissatisfied than the average person, who is content to pretend infallibility. The best thinkers are the most vigilant about their tendency to error; this vigilance is one of the characteristics that make them effective. This chapter explores this and other important habits, attitudes, and values associated with excellence in thinking. The more fully you understand these characteristics, the more successful you'll be in improving your thinking.

Qualities of a Thinking Person

A SCIENTIFIC ATTITUDE

It has become fashionable to believe that truth is subjective rather than objective and each individual finds it not by looking at external reality but by looking inward. Put more simply, the idea is that whatever we choose to believe is "true for us" and therefore beyond dispute. You've undoubtedly heard this expressed often enough that it seems reasonable, but let's test it and decide whether it really *is* reasonable. Some years ago, two brothers, Lyle and Eric Menendez, were indicted and tried (separately) for murdering their parents. The juries were unable to reach a verdict, partly because some jurors decided to believe that the young men couldn't have committed such an act, *even though they admitted in court to the shootings.* In other words, those jurors ignored the evidence presented in the courtroom and manufactured their own "truth." If we apply the popular view of truth, they acted properly! If that notion were extended throughout the court system, evidence would mean whatever each person wanted it to mean; thus there could be no standard of legal judgment. Further, courtroom testimony would become meaningless as would physical evidence. The victim's blood on the clothing of the accused, the murder weapon in his pocket, the eyewitnesses who saw him commit the crime could actually be considered compelling arguments for his *innocence* if someone decided to see them that way. And anyone who criticized that reasoning would be committing an offense.

The popular idea that truth is subjective doesn't make any more sense when applied to other subjects. It reduces the conclusions of the most painstaking scientific research to the level of one more viewpoint, no more credible than the muddled notions of the village ignoramus. It makes a mockery of every important distinction valued by scholars—accuracy versus inaccuracy, mindfulness versus mindlessness, rationality versus irrationality, informed judgment versus uninformed, profundity versus shallowness, mediocrity versus excellence, wisdom versus nonsense. It also trivializes scholarly processes: If insights into reality are found merely by peering into our own minds, what then is the purpose of archaeologists digging in the ground, historians sorting out the testimony of the past, medical researchers conducting laborious experiments, or sociologists probing the impact of culture on individuals?

The scientific attitude stands in stark contrast to the subjectivist view. It asserts that truth about the world outside ourselves is found by studying not our personal fancy or preference but the world outside ourselves. Equally important, it affirms that the process of finding the truth about anything is characterized not by invention but discovery. We discover truth by looking closely at the facts surrounding the matter in question, using appropriate investigative approaches and/or tools (for example, a laboratory procedure to test chemical reactions, a telescope to view the heavens). The scientific attitude also endorses what logicians call the principle of contradiction—*an idea that cannot be both true and false at the same time under the same circumstances*—and its corollary—*if an idea is true, its opposite is false.* (If an idea is only partly true, of course, the opposite idea may also be partly true.) Far from being an infringement on any perceived right to think as we wish, the principle of contradiction is a valuable guide to wisdom, enabling us to proceed with assurance that careful observation and thought make a difference.

Expressed in the most practical terms, the scientific attitude is the awareness that for every question there is one right answer—that is, one answer that is more accurate and more complete than all others—and the conviction that the right answer is worth pursuing, even if it takes years or centuries of effort to obtain it. Some right answers are achieved at once and confirmed by subsequent investigations. However, many others are preceded by wrong answers. For example, textbooks asserted for decades that African Americans played little or no role in the settling of the American West. More recent scholarship, however, suggests that such assertions were in error, documenting that one in every four cowboys in Texas cattle drives was African

American, as were *three in five* of the original settlers of Los Angeles (Minerbrook, 1994, p. 53).

Some issues are so complex or so far beyond the measuring capacity of our instruments or processes that many more generations will pass before their mysteries will be penetrated. But that situation in no way lessens the scientific conviction that there is a reality to be measured and one description of that reality will ultimately prove to be superior to all others. That conviction explains scientists' dedication to research and their commitment to informed, responsible discussion and debate.

AWARENESS OF THE LIMITS OF OPINION

The word "opinion" has two distinct meanings. One is *personal preference in matters of taste*. The kind of music or art we find pleasurable, the leisure activities we enjoy, our standard of beauty, and the features we prize in an automobile are examples of personal preferences. It is pointless to argue about such opinions because they essentially say "I like this" or "I don't like that" and no official standard can be invoked to settle the dispute. The second meaning of opinion is *conclusions about matters of judgment*. These include assessments of people, interpretations of events, and analyses of issues—in other words, any situation in which we use reasoning. Unlike matters of taste, matters of judgment can be evaluated for logic and/or conformity to the evidence.

The most common error about opinion is to confuse taste and judgment, believing that because taste is highly individualistic and beyond criticism, judgment must be too. This error is present when someone responds to a challenge to his or her judgment by saying "I'm entitled to my opinion," implying that having a right to an opinion guarantees that every opinion will be right. It is possible to exercise our constitutional guarantee of free speech and yet be totally wrong in what we say. At various times in history scholars believed that some insects came to life through "spontaneous generation," that the earth was the center of the solar system, that headaches are caused by demons inside the skull, and that women have smaller brains than men (even after allowing for the body-size differential). The people had a right to those opinions and were undoubtedly quite sincere in holding them. But that in no way alters the fact that all of those opinions were wrong.

CURIOSITY

Curiosity is a desire to know more about a subject or the world in general and is manifested in the habit of asking questions—how things got to be as they are, what relationships exist among ideas, where creativity could improve situations, why people react as they do and what their reactions signify, in how many different ways a problem or issue can be looked at, and so on. Where others take something for granted, curious people seek to become better acquainted with it. Little children tend to be very curious, adults less so, possibly because familiarity has dulled their sense of wonder. Regaining the curiosity of childhood can stimulate interest in learning, improve listening and observation skills, and increase one's store of knowledge.

One of the most profitable kinds of curiosity is wondering about the source of our ideas. It's pleasant to think that we derived all of our ideas by thinking carefully about the lessons our parents and teachers taught us, but that is not always the case. From early childhood, mass culture, including the media and the advertising industry, bombards us with ideas, many of them in conflict with those of home and school. Those ideas have a way of taking up residence in our minds and subtly but surely affecting our outlook. Each year the College Board compiles data on entering college freshmen. A generation ago, most students said that their main goal was to make a contribution to humankind, to make the world a better place to live. Today, most say their goal is to be well off financially. It is unlikely that such a change is attributable solely to parental teaching or the students' own careful analysis. The materialism of mass culture more likely exerted an unconscious influence on those students' thinking.

The process by which you became immersed in your culture and absorbed its values—good, bad, and questionable—is called *socialization*. Everyone undergoes it. Because the influences of this process are often so subtle that we do not recognize them, it follows that you can seldom be sure which of the ideas that now exist in your mind took up residence there without your informed consent. So you'll need to consider precisely how you've been affected by your family, teachers, friends, and celebrities and by the books you've read, the music you've listened to, and the television shows and films you've watched. Moreover, you should conduct such analysis not just about general influences but also about particular influences on the development of your most cherished convictions.

Some uninvited notions may have been with us so long that we treat them as our own creations, express them with the force of conviction, and feel honor bound to defend them against even token disagreement. If this idea strains belief, consider Swiss psychologist Jean Piaget's vivid recollection, from age 2 until 15, of his attempted kidnapping. He visualized sitting in his carriage, being taken for a walk by his nurse. Suddenly, a man tried to snatch him from the carriage. His nurse courageously fought the man off, receiving scratches during the struggle. In his memory Piaget could see the scratches on her face, the man fleeing, a policeman chasing him, and the crowd that gathered in the aftermath of the incident.

At age 15 Piaget learned that *the entire incident never happened.* His former nurse, feeling remorse for her duplicity, wrote his parents confessing that she had concocted the story to gain their favor (Piaget, 1991). Piaget had evidently heard the story many times and, after his imagination had elaborated on it, transformed it into a vivid memory.

The realization that such borrowed, untested, erroneous ideas are mixed in with your convictions is sobering. It needn't paralyze your thinking, but it should make you a little more humble and cognizant of your fallibility. Adopting the following perspective about your ideas will help you turn this realization to your benefit:

> I have absorbed thousands of ideas that I haven't had time to evaluate. Because they are in my mind, I may have expressed them often enough that I am convinced I conceived them. I dislike being so easily influenced; therefore, I will no longer regard an idea as my own just because it's in my mind or because I have expressed it. I will consider it my own only after I have studied it carefully, compared it with competing ideas, and decided it is the best one. And I will be ready to revise my view whenever one of my ideas proves to be flawed.

THE DESIRE AND EFFORT TO IMPROVE

One of the most important characteristics underlying all achievement is desire. Mastering the art of thinking, like quitting smoking, losing weight, and developing a power serve, depends on the strength of one's intention. Unfortunately, a major contemporary influence tends to block the desire, or weaken the resolve, to improve—the notion, unfortunately promoted in books and on television talk shows, that mental health demands "unconditional acceptance of ourselves," which implies that we ought to be satisfied in every respect with who and what we are. The now unfashionable traditional view is very different: It advises us to accept what is acceptable about ourselves and reject what is not. This view is more consistent with self-improvement because it encourages the dissatisfaction that will motivate you to change.

Socrates' well-known admonition "know thyself" can assist you in discovering appropriate dissatisfaction with yourself. (His related admission "I know nothing except the fact of my ignorance" suggests the value of intellectual humility.) Who you are is not just a biological matter but also a psychological and social matter. In the biological sense and, generally speaking, in the psychological sense, you have certain defining characteristics—all your genetically determined characteristics, your unique combination of experiences, feelings, and thoughts, and your acquired habits of mind. In contrast, the sociological self—the assortment of roles you have adopted in response to social situations—is far less constant. This self may differ, sometimes quite dramatically, from situation to situation. As a teenager, you undoubtedly behaved differently with your friends than you did with your parents or teachers. Your manner of speaking and acting was surely not the same in the locker room as it was in the classroom or in church. Today, you probably are to some extent a different person with your spouse than with your children, with your coworkers than with the boss.

You developed these multiple selves not because of any schizophrenic tendency but because the various situations presented you with different demands. You learned to react not only to people but to their expectations and the prevailing customs and conventions; you became sensitive to the symbols of those demands, the messages and cues that convey them. Sociologists call this response *symbolic interaction*. Each situation offers you a role of some sort, which you may accept or reject, with varying consequences. As the circumstances of your life change, your roles change. You marry, for example, and learn the role of spouse; you have children and struggle with the challenges of parenthood; you receive a promotion to supervisor and learn the protocols of your new position. In this way, your repertoire of behaviors toward other individuals and groups undergoes many changes.

One helpful way to achieve self-knowledge is to continually monitor your ignorance. Doing so makes you cautious in your assertions and on guard against the seductiveness of the familiar, the false assumption that hearing something makes it so. Another approach is to scrutinize your thinking processes. As interesting as it is to focus criticism on others' thought patterns and ideas, it is more beneficial to direct your analysis at yourself, to know *your* biases, predispositions, and triggers to irrationality. Everyone has them. Admitting you do is the first step in controlling them.

Self-evaluation also helps you resist the three major forms of manipulation—the exploitation of gullibility (e.g., people selling you things you don't need); the societal pressure to think, speak, and behave according to the latest fashion; and unrelieved self-congratulation, entertaining only thoughts that flatter and soothe your ego. This last kind is the worst because it deceives you into thinking that your opinions enjoy official status and expecting that others should pay them homage.

Here are some specific questions that will reveal valuable knowledge about your habits of mind. Ask them now to identify areas in which you can use improvement. Raise the most relevant ones again from time to time to check your progress at self-improvement:

- When I encounter a controversy, do I carefully weigh each side or do I immediately agree with one? Does my reaction depend on the particular controversy, the people engaged in discussing it, or some other factor?

- Do I periodically test my important ideas to be sure they are sound?

- What is my attitude toward change? Do I generally regard it favorably or unfavorably? Do I favor change in certain areas but not in others? (A strong feeling for or against change can cause uncritical acceptance or rejection of ideas, particularly if you are unaware of this tendency.)

- Am I a better thinker at certain times of the day? In certain circumstances? If so, which?

- How do I react when I encounter an idea I've never heard expressed before?

- Am I interested in others' perspectives or content to focus on my own? Am I interested in their views about some subjects but not about others? If so, which am I interested in and which disinterested in?

- Which of my important judgments about people or social institutions are based on my feelings or intuitions and which on careful accumulation of evidence?

- What situations do I find intimidating? What makes me react that way to those situations?

- How long am I able to concentrate without getting impatient and having my attention wander (e.g., when reading or listening to a lecture)?

- When is the last time I changed my mind about an important matter? What made me change it? Did I express the fact that I had changed it to anyone else? Why or why not?

- Do I ever go out of my way to read a book or article written by someone I know in advance does not share my view? If so, when is the last time I did so? If not, what are my reasons for not doing so?

- Have I ever pretended to be knowledgeable—to others or to myself—about a subject I know little or nothing about? If so, when is the last time this occurred?

WILLINGNESS TO ACKNOWLEDGE MISTAKES

Admitting to ourselves that we have been wrong is uncomfortable. That is why, in the words of James H. Robinson, "most of our so-called reasoning consists in finding arguments for going on believing as we already do." The following example illustrates how this can happen.

Ralph has long been aware that the 1973 *Roe v. Wade* decision of the U.S. Supreme Court declared that women have a constitutional right to choose whether they will continue a pregnancy and that the fetus is not considered a person and thus enjoys no rights under the law. Like many Americans, Ralph considers the issue legally settled and regards pro-life arguments as purely religious and totally without legal merit. Recently, Ralph became aware that since 1975 the Constitutional Court of Germany has held the exactly opposite legal view—that "the life of each individual human being is self-evidently a central value of the legal order . . . [and] the constitutional duty to protect this life also includes its preliminary stages before birth"—and moreover that the German high court reaffirmed this view in 1993, holding that the state has "a duty to place itself protectively before unborn human life, shielding this life from unlawful attacks" and calling for penal laws against anyone who would pressure pregnant women into having abortions" (cited in Arkes, 1994, p. 16).

Because these facts suggest very clearly that Ralph's conclusion about pro-life arguments was wrong, honesty demands that Ralph acknowledge to himself that he was mistaken, that the pro-life position is not only a religious view but a legitimate legal perspective. This admission does not require that he give up his pro-choice position or that he declare to another living soul that he was wrong in his assessment. Even so, he will probably be tempted to pretend his view needs no changing. With a modest expenditure of imagination, he can reason (ludicrously) that the German legal system doesn't count or that American jurisprudence trumps foreign jurisprudence. If he entertains this idea long enough, or repeats it to himself often enough, he may even come to believe it. That's the pathetic truth about us humans—we're often willing to go to almost any lengths, even to embrace asinine notions, rather than admit to error.

The issue is not merely one of integrity. It makes no sense to go on believing something that, in light of new evidence, we know to be false. To do so is to condemn ourselves to imprisonment in error for an indeterminate sentence. The best thinkers avoid punishing themselves in this way. Knowing that no one bats a thousand in thinking any more than in baseball, they expect to be wrong a fair share of the time. Accordingly, they remain alert for new evidence and ready to reopen previously settled issues.

A POSITIVE REGARD FOR CONVICTIONS

The various cautions expressed so far in this chapter about the possibility of error may seem to imply that anyone who aspires to excellence in thinking should resist the urge to form convictions. Some educated people have, in fact, reached that conclusion, believing that having convictions disqualifies one as an analyst. They are mistaken. The essential aim of thinking, after all, is to distinguish sound ideas from unsound ideas. A person who goes to the considerable trouble of surveying ideas without embracing any is no different from one who carefully sorts worthless rocks from semiprecious stones and semiprecious stones from precious gems—and then throws them all away. The proper descriptor for such a person is not wise but foolish.

Thoughtful sociologists, like thoughtful chemists, literary critics, accountants, or gardeners, may have many convictions—about the value of their disciplines, about the trustworthiness of their methods, and about the validity of those (admittedly few) research findings that have time and again stood the test of professional scrutiny and replication. True, all these thoughtful people will on occasion be proved wrong, but that no more impugns the value of convictions than failed relationships disprove the value of love. The danger is not having convictions but falling victim to the delusion of infallibility and refusing to submit them to the process of review and revision applicable to other ideas.

Simply said, the best advice for anyone who aspires to excellence in thinking is "Don't be afraid to form convictions—just do so with care and don't etch them in stone."

FAIRMINDEDNESS

Much has been written about the danger of bias affecting judgments. Some go so far as to maintain that bias is inescapable and hopelessly corrupts all analysis and judgment. That assessment oversimplifies the matter. There are really two kinds of bias: the hard variety, *prejudice*, which predetermines the outcome of the investigation, allowing little if any room for alteration; and the soft variety, *predilection*, the more modest tilting of the mind caused by prior experience, opinion, some other form of allegiance (e.g., religious or political belief), or intellectual temperament. Practically speaking, hard bias does hopelessly corrupt judgment; its only antidote is enlightenment to the error of prejudice. Soft bias, however, is often benign and can be balanced by fairmindedness.

Fairmindedness means being sportsmanlike with ideas, giving each a chance to prove itself and not using a double standard that accepts glaring faults in the ideas of people who agree with us and ignores insights in the ideas of those who disagree. (Lack of fairmindedness is, alas, all too common; see, e.g., Sherman & Kunda, 1989, cited in Wade, 1993.) More than just a requirement of etiquette, fairmindedness is based on these important realities: Everyone is capable of error; generally, in complex issues the truth does not lie entirely on either side of the argument; and familiar views often seem superior even when they are not. To be fairminded in your analyses, recognize the way your mind is tilting on the issue and go out of your way to consider the merits of the other side.

OPENNESS TO DISAGREEMENT AND CRITICISM

For many of us, even mild disagreement with our ideas is perceived as harsh criticism. That is understandable; at some level, unconsciously at least, we expect other people to love our ideas as we do. Anything less than that we interpret as a mark of disrespect for us. But because such criticism may not be disrespectful at all but merely a mark of their respect for logic and the pursuit of truth, reasonableness demands that we overcome our resentment and see the benefits of criticism—it keeps us on our intellectual toes, is a source of insight into the strengths and weaknesses of our ideas, and can stimulate our thinking if we allow it to. The following strategies will help you receive disagreement and criticism in the right spirit.

Acknowledge your "mine is better" attitude. Everyone develops this attitude in childhood, when we tend to regard our parents, our tricycles, our pets, and so on as better than anyone else's. Admittedly, abusive parents or impoverished circumstances may prompt a "mine is worse" attitude. Likewise, it is possible, in spite of good or even privileged circumstances, to *envy* someone else's situation. But even in such situations, virtually everyone will feel "mine is better" about something. And as time dims our recollections of the fears and frustrations of childhood, nostalgia can extend a "mine is better" feeling to the times and places and associations of our entire youth.

In most people, maturity tempers the "mine is better" attitude—they come to realize that others feel the same way about the important people and things in their lives, that such feelings are a mixture of genuine affection and egotism ("Mine must be better because I *am special*"). Yet remnants of "mine is better" tend to remain no matter how educated and insightful we become and are most evident in our attitude toward our ideas. Those who agree with our point of view we tend to regard as astute, penetrating thinkers; those who disagree we consider intellectually deficient. Careful thinkers regard this tendency in themselves with a little amusement and a lot of control. When it surfaces, they say to themselves "My mind is at it again playing that little ego game" and redouble their effort to give opposing ideas a fair hearing. They do this not just because it's good etiquette but because they aren't satisfied with *pretending* to have the most reasonable ideas; they want to *have* them, and they're willing to pay the price.

Accept the burden of proof. The act of making an assertion entails the responsibility of defending it if challenged. When someone is not content to accept without question something you've written or expressed in discussion and asks you why you think as you do or what evidence supports your position, don't take offense—such questions are legitimate. It is not up to other people to refute your assertions (although refutation is an option that is open to them); the burden of proof for your assertions is yours. And you will meet it best by anticipating it in advance, thus being prepared to answer any question about your idea even before you express that idea.

Control your defense mechanisms. Defense mechanisms are dishonest strategies for refusing to deal with challenges to your ideas or to realities about which you feel uncomfortable. Perhaps the most common of these mechanisms is *denial*, pretending not to have said what you actually said or that something did not occur when it actually did. Historically, many men have met charges of inequality to women with denial. Another common defense mechanism is *rationalization*, beginning with the desired conclusion and then selectively accumulating evidence that supports it (rather than consulting all the evidence and forming the conclusion accordingly).[1] An example of rationalization is radical feminists' assertion that all men are rapists and even acts of consensual sex, as for example in marriage, are acts of rape: As many commentators, including many moderate feminists, have noted, these writers clearly began with their conclusion and "massaged" the evidence to fit it. A third common defense mechanism is *projection*, whereby one experiences hostile feelings toward one's critics and then accuses the critics of harboring those feelings.

Avoid explaining away evidence and attacking others. The easiest way to dispose of an unwanted criticism is to explain it away. This is usually done either by dismissing it as irrelevant to the issue, even though it is relevant, or by acknowledging its relevance but classifying it as unimportant, even though it is important. Attacking others (known in logic as the *ad hominem* fallacy) means shifting the discussion from the issue to the person who challenged one's idea. It is an error because pointing out someone's personal failings does not refute his or her argument. Even a scoundrel may, on occasion, advance a sound argument or make a valid criticism; likewise, the most honorable people can be mistaken. Both explaining away evidence and attacking others are dishonest tactics.

To ensure that you remain open to criticism and maintain your integrity in writing and/or speaking, follow these approaches:

- When you are engaged in solving a problem or analyzing an issue, take care that the assertions you make are factual and the conclusions you draw are the most reasonable ones in light of the evidence. (Consider all possible conclusions before embracing any one.)
- When any of your views, even cherished ones, are challenged by another person or by new evidence, don't react defensively. Remind your-

self that truth is more important than ego and reevaluate the matter fairmindedly.

INQUIRY

Save your response to the following inquiry. You will need to refer back to it to complete a future assignment.

■ Evaluate yourself on each of the qualities discussed in the chapter. Identify which areas you are weakest in and make a note to work on these throughout the course. (Don't despair if your list is fairly extensive; most people have a number of areas that need improvement.)

Note

1. The definition of rationalization offered here is one that logicians use. Some sociologists, notably Max Weber, define the term very differently, as elaboration of cultural principles (as in development of a complex theoretical system) or social organization (as in development of bureaucracies).

3

❧

Thinking Reflectively

Reflective thinking, as noted in Chapter 1, is a blend of observation and wonder that serves to identify matters worthy of closer analysis. Every theory, concept, perspective, and method is fair game for reflection. The value of this kind of thinking is best appreciated by understanding two realities: first, that knowledge can always be widened and deepened, and secondly, that nothing of human invention is ever perfect—everything can be improved. Thus, if the subject of reflection chosen is worthy of attention, your effort will always be rewarded with no less than additional knowledge and occasionally with an exciting insight that others may have missed. W.E.B. DuBois' curiosity about the conditions of life in African-American urban centers led him to conduct his well-known survey. Robert Merton's curiosity about social and economic influences on scientific investigation produced the doctoral dissertation that launched a distinguished career and contributed important advances to the sociology of science.

From time to time throughout this century, the public has become concerned that a "crime wave" was sweeping the land. Sociologist Mark Fishman (1995) became curious about this phenomenon and decided to investigate the "waves of [media] coverage of some topic in crime" (p. 43). Examining the way the job of reporting and editing is done, he found that crime waves are created when journalists present individual crimes as specific incidents of a recurring theme. Themes, he learned, are helpful tools in sorting data from wire services, press releases, and reports from police and other public and private agencies. Although there must be enough incidents that fit the theme for the story to be sustained, Fishman concluded that *newsworthiness is determined more by the theme than by the details of the story.* One reason why crime in the streets is a defining factor in the crime wave and white-collar crime is not, he asserts, is that the daily police summary provides a constant supply of the former. Once the crime wave is widely reported, journalists can capitalize on another rich source of news material—"the responses of politicians, police, and other officials" (p. 47).

How can you ensure that your reflection will yield the payoffs gained by the researchers in these examples? Unfortunately, no one has yet devised a foolproof system and the likelihood that someone will do so is on the order of finding a foolproof system for winning the lottery. But even the small prize in reflective thinking—increased understanding—is more than worth the effort. The effectiveness of your creative and critical thinking will depend on the quality of your reflective thinking—before you can generate and evaluate ideas, you must first select an issue.

Promising Areas for Reflection

Even though no area of inquiry is guaranteed to be fruitful, a number of them have proved to be especially promising. Focusing on them will increase your chances of achieving both understanding and insight.

THE NEGLECTED SIDE OF CONTROVERSIAL ISSUES

A controversy is, by definition, an issue about which informed and intelligent people are divided, and, therefore, each side will usually have some validity. However, for some perverse reason, we humans have a tendency to regard controversies as having only one defensible side and, no surprise, that side is the one we favor. The communication media, at least in part because of time and space limitations, often manage to neglect one side of an issue, and (still no surprise) the neglected one is almost always the unpopular side or the one that challenges the reigning media viewpoint. Neglect may take the form of totally ignoring one viewpoint, but more commonly it consists of underreporting or unrepresentative reporting, falsely implying that only eccentrics endorse that view. However tempting it might be to conclude that some media conspiracy underlies such neglect, it is much more reasonable to ascribe it to unconscious bias. In any case, the effort to identify and examine the neglected side of controversies can provide you with interesting ideas for reflection.

To illustrate, consider a matter which popular culture has treated in such a one-sided fashion that it is widely and uncritically accepted as fact—the view of the self. In that view, the self is good and, in the interests of emotional health, should be accepted without reservation. In popular parlance, we should all practice "unconditional self-acceptance" so that we will be filled with "self-esteem." Chances are you've encountered one or more professional people who warn of the dangers of low self-esteem and an even greater number of celebrities who regale talk-show audiences with accounts of the wonderful effects that have resulted from their learning to love themselves. Innumerable books and articles have been written from this point of view. Self-esteem philosophy has become the dominant psychothera-peutic and educational theory.

The realization that millions of people have evidently accepted this view, apparently unquestioningly, would be your trigger for re-flection. "Wait a minute," you'd say, "isn't this all a little too pat? Is every self really that wonderful? What about _____ and _____? [Here you'd fill in the names of people—we all know some—whose lovableness, if it exists at all, is well hidden.] Isn't it likely that this concept of the self met with some opposition from responsible scholars? Why haven't I heard the dissenters, as-suming there are any? Is it perhaps because they've been passed over by the talk shows and their books have been kept in the less promi-nent sections of the bookstores?"

Here, for example, is the view of one dissenter, Paul C. Vitz (1994):

> The basic assumption of humanistic selfism—namely the complete goodness of human nature (as opposed to the evil influence from so-ciety)—receives extremely strong criticisms from a wide variety of sci-entists and support from remarkably few. The humanists' central concept of the conscious self is poorly defined, filled with contradic-tions, and seriously inadequate both as a description of our psycho-logical nature and as a tool for serious psychotherapy. Self-theory psychology has not shown the systematic development of a traditional science, in which replicated findings and increasingly precise concepts lead one generation to build on the work of the other. Instead, self-theories have turned into popular and commercialized ideologies with concepts that are even more vague and diffuse than those of forty years ago. . . . In short, humanistic selfism is not a science but a popular secular substitute religion, which has nourished and spread today's widespread cult of self-worship. (pp. 140-141)

Writing from a similar perspective, James Hitchcock (1982) appraises the impact of self-absorption on Western society as follows:

> Popular culture over the past twenty years has exhorted men to exalt themselves, cater to themselves, almost to adore themselves. Yet the result has been that people have sunk deeper and deeper into moral

and spiritual confusion and social breakdown. The formulas proclaimed to exalt men and make them happy have led to debasement and cynicism. (p. 150)

Will the neglected side of this issue prove more or less insightful than the popularly accepted side? At this stage of your thinking, it's too early to tell. But by raising questions and stimulating reflection you've turned an apparently settled matter into an adventure and, in Sherlock Holmes' famous phrase, "the game's afoot."

POPULAR IDEAS THAT ARE
SELDOM, IF EVER, CRITICIZED

Research reveals that the more often we hear an idea expressed, the more likely we are to accept it as true. We're not speaking here of an argument on behalf of an idea or the presentation of evidence, just the mere statement and repetition of the idea (Arkes, 1991). Research also reveals that most people will contradict the findings of their senses, at least on occasion, in order to gain the security of agreeing with others (Asch, 1952, 1965). In combination, these two tendencies constitute a powerful capacity for error; therefore, popular ideas that are seldom criticized represent a promising subject for reflection.

For at least a couple of decades it was widely assumed that certain kinds of behavior are linked to one or the other gender—for example, women were considered nurturing and men nonnurturing. Then, sociologist Barbara Risman (1987) wondered whether that view was accurate. She compared personality traits of single fathers, single mothers, and married parents and found that single fathers, when caring for children, displayed the traits of nurturance thought to be feminine traits. There was nothing special about these men; they had the responsibility of caring for their children for a variety of reasons, mainly the death or desertion of their wives or the wives' decision not to share custody. Risman concluded that the traits in question are as dependent on the tasks being performed as on one's gender. Subsequent studies of men in roles that demanded nurturing, such as caring for their aged parents or ailing wives, confirmed Risman's findings.

In 1982, Carol Gilligan published *In a Different Voice*, in which she argued that women differ from men in their approach to moral decisions: Women employ principles of compassion and caring; for men, it's abstract reasoning about justice. Immediately accepted as a breakthrough idea, Gilligan's view caused a reexamination of the field of ethics and of ethical reasoning in every discipline. But some scholars wondered whether writers, journalists, politicians, and even scholars had jumped on the bandwagon too uncritically. Because of their willingness to retain their curiosity about an issue that many regarded as settled, a very different view has emerged. According to Carol Tavris (1992), "Research in recent years casts considerable doubt on the notion that men and women differ appreciably in their moral reasoning, or that women have a permanently different voice because of their early closeness to their mothers" (p. 83).

Like other Americans, scholars as well as laypeople, Edith Gomberg observed the 1980s' phenomenon of "codependency" in its rapid unfolding. Many books were written, some achieving bestsellerdom. Recovery groups like Codependents Anonymous and Adult Children of Alcoholics sprang up to teach relatives how to cope with the problem and to avoid being "enablers." The subject was featured on television talk shows and quickly spilled over from its original category of alcoholism to drug addiction and then to many other situations characterized by out-of-control behavior. Then Edith Gomberg wondered about what kind and quality of data supported the codependence movement. She researched the published literature and found . . . NOTHING! In her words, *"There are no surveys, no clinical research, no evaluations; only descriptive, impressionistic statements"* (cited in Tavris, 1992, p. 199; emphasis added).

These examples should not be taken to suggest that analysis will expose most popular ideas to be in error. You may, in fact, find that very few are. The point is that you will never know unless you wonder.

APPARENT CONTRADICTIONS AND ABSURDITIES

Some of the same politicians who proclaim that the family is the cornerstone of society and talk about the importance of restoring it to a position of importance support tax laws that penalize married people and welfare programs that discourage fathers from living in the home. Some commentators on America's social problems say that young people should challenge authority and assert their own "truth" about reality and then chastise teachers for not maintaining discipline in the classroom. Many New Age religionists reject Christianity and Judaism as unscientific and proceed to embrace channeling 35,000-year-old beings from other "dimensions," healing with crystals, prophesying with Tarot cards, and astrology. Publishers, seeing many people content to be mediocre and dismissive of hard work and responsibility, offer the public books on the dangers of workaholism. Each of these cases is an example of apparent contradiction that begs to be examined and resolved.

As great as the logical tension in apparent contradictions is, it is even greater in outright absurdities. Amazingly, some absurdities manage to escape detection, occasionally for years. An example of one that has continued to swell for almost a decade concerns "dysfunctional families." Several years ago, it reached the point where some argued that as many as 96% of American families qualify for the dubious distinction (see Tavris, 1992, p. 173). Long before the total became inflated to this extent, everyone who values logic should have wondered "When dysfunction becomes the norm, doesn't it *cease to be* dysfunction?" and proceeded to reexamine the concept.

A note of caution is in order here: Not every apparent contradiction or absurdity is an *actual* one. The assertion "Sometimes the best way to improve your performance is to forget about performing" may seem ludicrous at first consideration, but many actors, dancers, and athletes attest to its wisdom. For the purposes under discussion here, the appearance of logical conflict should be considered not as proof of contradiction but as an invitation to reflection.

VENERATED THEORIES AND
RESEARCH PERSPECTIVES

Say what? If they are venerated, doesn't that mean they are beyond suspicion? Not at all. It merely means that they have been regarded as venerable; that is not the same as being venerable. Remember the story about the emperor's new clothes? With one exception, everyone in the kingdom embraced the illusion that the emperor had new clothes. The one who looked at the data independently saw that the king was naked. How can scholars be fooled in this manner? Rowland W. Jepson (1967) gave a partial answer:

A statement of opinion by one writer may be re-stated as a fact by another, who may in turn be quoted as an authority by yet another; and this process may continue indefinitely, unless it occurs to someone to question the facts on which the original writer based his opinion or to challenge the interpretation he placed upon those facts. (p. 123)

Of course, Jepson wasn't speaking specifically about scholars. Does it ever happen that *scholars* will pass on erroneous notions and other *scholars* will endorse those notions so that in time they achieve the level of undisputed truth? Although such a phenomenon is not commonplace, it has been known to occur. And the process is easiest when the *zeitgeist*, the spirit of the age, is amenable to the idea, thus assuring its dissemination. In our time, a number of questionable ideas may be cited to illustrate this phenomenon.

The concept of mental illness enjoys a long and distinguished history and continues to be almost universally accepted in psychiatry. Yet psychiatrist Thomas Szasz (1990) has advanced a provocative scholarly challenge to it (as well as to the related concept of insanity). Although it is impossible here to do justice to his argument in its fullness, the following brief statement suggests that it is an interesting argument worthy of thoughtful consideration:

Psychiatrists and all those steeped in the psychiatric ideology take the decisive initial step of omitting to define illness in general, or bodily illness in particular, and instead *define mental illness* (whatever they mean by it) *as a member of the class called illness.* I reject this approach. Instead of accepting the phenomena called mental illnesses as diseases, the decisive initial step I take is to *define illness as the pathologist defines it—as a structural or functional abnormality of cells, tissues, organs, or bodies.* If the phenomena called mental illnesses manifest themselves as such structural or functional abnormalities, then they are *diseases;* if they do not, they are *not.* Unless we exercise such candor, we shall stand in perpetual danger of confusing definition with discovery. (p. 12)

Another venerated theory is that human needs exist in a hierarchy, with self-actualization at the pinnacle. This idea was advanced by Abraham Maslow in the form of a pyramid. From base to peak, the needs he specified are (a) physiological (food, shelter, and clothing), (b) belongingness and love, (c) self-esteem, (d) aesthetic and cognitive (intellectual), and (e) self-actualization. According to Maslow, all the lower needs must be met, each in its turn, before the higher ones can be fulfilled. Note that self-esteem must be met before aesthetic and cognitive needs. (This explains why many educators feel it essential to address self-esteem before they address academic content.) Note, too, that in this scheme *all* lower needs must be met before self-actualization can be accomplished.

Given a modest effort, even people who lack scholarly credentials could raise some interesting questions about Maslow's theory: Are these all the needs, or are there some he didn't identify? Does the use of a standard pyramid, rather than an upside-down one or a circle, unduly affect our perception of the process? Must the relationship be hierarchical? Could the needs be concurrent? Might some be concurrent and others hierarchical? Are the categories in the most realistic order—in other words, might not self-esteem be at the pinnacle, to be reached only after and *through* aesthetic and cognitive pursuits and self-actualization? Might self-actualization be not a need at all but something else—for example, a technique for fulfilling certain needs?

Some scholars have, in fact, raised certain of these questions, among others. A Dutch researcher, for example, has concluded that Maslow's hierarchy doesn't always hold true in other countries. He points out that in Belgium, Greece, and Japan job security is often a greater need than self-actualization and that the need for affiliation and acceptance is greater than self-actualization in some Scandinavian countries (Hofstede, 1988; see also Howell & Dipboye, 1986). But the most telling criticism has come from the distinguished Austrian psychiatrist, Viktor Frankl (1978).[1]

The most human of needs, Frankl asserts, is not self-actualization but self-*transcendence* (p. 35). A person becomes fully human "by forgetting himself and giving himself, overlooking himself and focusing outward" (p. 67). Making self-actualization (or happiness) the direct object of our pursuit, Frankl argues, is ultimately self-defeating; such fulfillment can occur only as "the unintended effect of self-transcendence" (p. 83).

Even Kinsey's studies on male and female sexuality, arguably among the most far-reaching of all scholarly works in terms of their impact on social institutions, has been challenged in recent years. Judith A. Reisman and Edward W. Eichel (1990) meticulously analyzed the two works and documented some shocking charges, including the following: that Kinsey knowingly used biased samples and that he tolerated, and perhaps encouraged, the sexual molestation of children for his studies, the most disturbing example being the oral and manual stimulation to orgasm of several hundred infants and children by a group of nine sex offenders.

Reisman and Eichel further document that Kinsey approached his studies with a clear personal agenda that influenced his findings. His goals, they point out, were to establish that exclusive heterosexuality is abnormal and results merely from conditioning and inhibitions; that sex between a man and a woman is no more natural than sex between two men, a man and a child, or a man and an animal; and that bisexuality should be the norm in human sexual expression. The authors also cite that Abraham Maslow had demonstrated to Kinsey that the approach he was using was unscientific, yet Kinsey ignored him and used the approach anyway. The data resulting from that approach led to Kinsey's published conclusion that incest can be satisfying and enriching and that the only reason why children get upset from sexual contact with adults is because of the prudishness of parents and legal authorities.

The findings of these researchers can be verified by reading the specified passages in Kinsey. The amazing thing is that these facts could have been missed by so many scholars for over four decades—a classic case, it would seem, of the emperor's new clothes syndrome.

Getting Started With Reflection

If you don't feel completely comfortable addressing issues of the magnitude of Maslow's hierarchy of needs or the concept of insanity, don't be concerned. That's a normal reaction. Just begin developing your reflective thinking with smaller challenges. You'll find plenty if you focus your curiosity on everyday activities. Begin with your textbooks (all of them, not just sociology). For example, if you read about one of the studies that enlisted whites who were prejudiced toward blacks to work with blacks, or play sports with them, or tutor together for a period of several weeks, you'll note that the prejudice of the whites was sharply reduced as a result. Instead of accepting that and reading on, consider what a professional researcher might ask about that study, what other questions it left unanswered. One researcher wondered whether the reduction in prejudice applied to just the activity in the study or whether it transferred to other activities. Pursuing the question, he found that it did *not* necessarily transfer (see See & Wilson, 1988, p. 228).

Take note of the ideas, attitudes, and values revealed in discussions with your family, friends, and acquaintances. And be attentive to what people talk about on the bus or subway or in the cafeteria.

Look, too, at what's reported in the news, in the opinions expressed on editorial pages of newspapers, and in magazines and journals. For example, if you heard Oprah announce in September 1994 that she had had enough victims on her show and would no longer include such programming, you might have asked, "Is it possible that by having so many assorted victims on their shows Oprah and the other talk-show hosts aggravated the problem of 'victimitis'?" Be aware of what is being talked about and debated among intelligent people, what books are on the best-seller list, what music is topping the charts, and what's being covered in the tabloids. Yes, the tabloids. You'll find lots of ideas there too, although generally of a different quality than the ideas found in more respectable newspapers.

Television is an especially rich source because it reaches more people than any other entertainment or communication medium. Moreover, according to sociologist Gaye Tuchman (1988), researchers have found that

> audience members often react to actors (comedians, musicians, and others featured in the media) as though they had a personal relationship with them. This tendency is most often pronounced in the case of television audiences . . . and so may make information on television seem more personally compelling than information gleaned from friends or acquaintances. (p. 604)

And researchers Ball and Rokeach have demonstrated that "television [has] induced long-range cognitive and behavioral effects in the daily lives of adults in the privacy of their own homes" (cited in Tuchman, 1988, p. 618).

Sociologist Todd Gitlin (1980) has used Antonio Gramsci's concept of *ideological hegemony* to explain how the media affect the public. Gitlin explains that the concept represents

> a ruling class's (or alliance's) domination of subordinate classes and groups through the elaboration and penetration of ideology (ideas and assumptions) into their common sense and everyday practice; it is the

s ystematic (but not necessarily or even usually deliberate) engineering
c f mass consent to the established order. (p. 253)

Moreover, Gitlin argues, "the hegemonic sense of the world seeps
into 'common sense' and get reproduced there; it may even appear
to be generated by that common sense" (p. 254).

If these ideas make you wonder about the legitimacy of the television industry's claim that it merely holds a mirror to reality and its
programming has no effect on the public, be assured that you are not
alone. For decades, researchers have conducted rigorous studies of
the effects of television viewing, and their conclusions have been
remarkably consistent. If you have not heard of them, it is only because the media have preferred to ignore them. Robert Liebert and
Joyce Sprafkin (1988) compiled and analyzed more than twenty years
of research studies. Here are just a few of the important points they
discuss:

- George Gerbner's conclusion that "one correlate of television viewing
  is a heightened and unequal sense of danger and risk in a mean and
  selfish world" (p. 149).
- The conclusion of Huesman's study of the relationship between expo-
  sure to TV violence at age 8 and the seriousness of criminal acts performed at age 30: "[E]arly television habits are in fact correlated with
  adult criminality" (p. 153).
- F. S. Andison's review of the findings of 67 separate studies, from which
  he concluded a correlation between viewing TV violence and behaving
  aggressively. Furthermore, the correlation was present despite differences in "research methods, age of subjects, measures of aggression,
  and time period and country of investigation" (pp. 155-156).
- S. Hearold's finding, in reviewing 230 separate studies, that research
  consistently demonstrates a relationship between antisocial behavior
  and the viewing of violent TV fare (p. 156).

Such findings also suggest questions about the effects of nonviolent programming—the talk shows, the dramatic programs, includ-

ing soap operas and miniseries, the game shows, the MTV videos, and the advertising appeals that punctuate all such programming.

A Potpourri of Sample Questions

What follows is a modest sample of the interesting sociological inquiries curiosity can prompt:

- Does ability to function intellectually (e.g., to make decisions) decline with age? If so, when does this decline tend to occur? What factors are associated with it? Does it depend on the circumstances/environment the person lives in? If so, can changing the circumstances/environment restore intellectual function?
- Has child abuse increased over the past couple of decades, or is it just better reported now?
- Do the poor receive different quality health care from that available to the middle class or the affluent? If so, is the difference explainable solely by economic factors? What other factors might be involved?
- What preferences do the various social classes and ethnic groups have in amateur/professional sports?
- How do men and women differ in their views on abortion, health care, or women in the military? Are there also differences between young men and older men and between young women and older women?
- Which of the following tend to be more politically conservative? Asian Americans, Caucasian Americans, Latino Americans, African Americans, Native Americans? What differences exist in each group by gender? By age?
- What sports do women under 30 enjoy watching? Participating in? What sports do women over 30 enjoy watching? Participating in?
- What have been the consequences of the increasing divorce rate over the past half-century? How have these consequences differed for husbands, wives, male children, and female children?
- What are the attitudes of teenagers toward retired people? Of working women? Of working men?

- Is there a difference among ethnic groups in the relationships of parents and adult children? Is there a difference between first-generation Americans and later generations?

- Is there any correlation between retirement and the incidence of illness, suicide, or divorce?

- What has been the impact of the social upheavals of the 1960s and 1970s?

- Has the involvement of younger children in violent crimes increased? If so, what factors have contributed to the increase?

- What percentage of children who commit violent crimes display remorse for their acts? How does this percentage compare with that of adult criminals? If there is a difference, to what might it be attributed?

- What is the average height of winning candidates in national elections? What is the average height of losing candidates?

- Why do journalists sit on current affairs analysis show panels? What are their qualifications? Does reporting the news about medicine or politics or social problems confer a level of expertise?

- Who appears on the major network morning shows and on the talk shows? What types of authors and entertainers are underrepresented? What subjects are most commonly aired?

Keeping a Journal

A journal is different from a notebook. A notebook is a record of information, not too selectively gathered from lectures and reading, for the purpose of passing an examination. When you enter data into a notebook, you usually have no intention of pondering them; your only purpose is having them available for review. A journal, on the other hand, is a record of ideas that are in themselves interesting and thus seem to merit closer inspection—you write them down *so that* you can reflect on them later. You may not have used a journal before, except perhaps in English class, but it is useful in any course, such as sociology, in which you wish to deepen your understanding and stimulate your thinking. To keep a journal, you first capture ideas and then, usually at a later time, reflect on their meaning and value.

CAPTURING IDEAS

Undoubtedly you've experienced having an interesting idea occur to you at an inconvenient time—say, when you are just about to fall asleep or while driving to class—and then being unable to remember it later. Similarly, you may hear someone express a thought that strikes you as insightful, and you tell yourself "As soon as I get a chance, I'm going to ponder that idea further." But when you get the chance, you've forgotten the idea or your reaction to it, or both. These experiences are common. The wisest approach is not to depend on memory but to write the ideas down immediately and, if appropriate, add a brief note about their significance or usefulness. By capturing them at once, you can be sure they will be available to you when you want them. You will also tend to become more observant and more inclined to *seek* meaning in your experiences.

The term "ideas," in the sense it is being used here, is broadly defined. It includes the following:

- Interpretations and/or conclusions drawn by authors, professors, or other people, including fellow students, about sociological data. (Because sociology has a larger area of focus than many other disciplines, "sociological data" may be found in other fields.)
- Judgments about the sufficiency of data.
- Past or present decisions about the appropriateness of investigative procedures or the ethical quality of actions.
- Arguments advanced for one sociological perspective or against another.
- Actual experiences you have had, have witnessed, or have heard or read about.
- Your own or other people's questions about any aspect of sociology. (For our purposes a question is as much an idea as an assertion is.)

The term "ideas" also covers all gradations of quality from the uniquely wise to the outrageously ludicrous and everything in between. Wise ideas are useful for the obvious reason; foolish ones are useful because they provide insight into the nature or process of error. Keep in mind, too, that an idea that *seems* wise may ultimately prove to be foolish and vice versa.

UNDERSTANDING IDEAS

To fulfill the aim of reflective thinking, you must not only write ideas down but also understand their relationship to other ideas and their potential impact within the discipline and, more broadly, in society. The way to reach such understanding is to ask and answer appropriate questions, many of which will depend on the specific nature of the idea. The following ones, however, have general application in sociology:

- Does this idea *support* any important aspect of sociology? For example, does it reinforce a principle or concept, clarify a definition or a procedure, or provide a helpful analogy?
- Does this idea *challenge* anything I have learned in sociology? If so, what does it challenge, and how does it challenge it?
- If the idea proves to be a valid insight, how will it impact on the field of sociology? What principles, concepts, perspectives, and approaches will it force to be revised?
- Does the idea suggest an interesting avenue of investigation, one that perhaps has not been adequately explored?
- What other subjects does it touch? Does it call into question anything that I or others believe, such as some fashionable, widely accepted "wisdom" of the day?

Here are five tips to help you use your journal effectively:

1. Don't combine your journal entries with your lecture notes—buy a separate notebook for your journal, preferably one with bound pages rather than a looseleaf or spiral-bound book.
2. Carry your journal with you wherever you go or, if that is not practical, jot down ideas on scrap paper and transfer them into your journal later.

3. Don't be self-conscious about making notes when other people are around. If someone should ask what you are writing, just say "something I don't want to forget."

4. Devote some time to your journal every day, even if you can spare no more than 15 minutes. Choose a time when you are not too tired and can put other concerns aside.

5. Use the left pages of the journal for capturing ideas and the right (facing) pages for examining them. Because examining requires more space, leave ample space between ideas as you record them.

Here's how the process of making an entry in your journal might proceed. You learn that the number of listings in the *Diagnostic and Statistical Manual of Mental Disorders* (*DSM*), published by the American Psychiatric Association, has ballooned from 60 kinds of mental illness in 1952 to 145 in 1968, 230 in 1987 and over 300 in 1994. Instead of just writing that information down, you pause and wonder. You look at the *DSM* and notice that the illnesses include Self-Defeating Personality, Parental Child Problem (example given: a "conflict between a mentally healthy adolescent and her parents about her choice of friends"), Academic Problem ("a pattern of failing grades"), Undifferentiated Attention-Deficit Disorder (symptoms: "persistence of developmentally inappropriate and marked inattention that is not a symptom of another disorder"), and Occupational Problem (a condition *not* due to mental disorder, such as "job dissatisfaction and uncertainty about career choices").

When time permits, make a brief entry in your journal, recording what you found, using only the left side of the page, together with the following questions: What can explain this inflation in the number of entries? Could so many new diseases have come into being during this time? If so, what caused them? Could the diseases have existed previously but not been discovered until recently? If so, what should be credited with the breakthrough? New diagnostic methods? Technological advances? Is it possible, instead, that psychiatrists have been redefining their field in a way that incorporates what used to be contained in other fields? What are the implications of such redefinition? Has the line between normal and abnormal been blurred or, in some cases, erased? (That would seem the only explanation for some of the illnesses noted above.) Does the inflation in *DSM* categories support or refute Dr. Szasz's (1990) contention about mental illness? (See pp. 42-43, this volume.)

The *DSM* example illustrates the value of a broad, as opposed to a narrow, interest in issues. Ignoring the increase in mental illness categories because it is a psychiatric issue rather than a sociological one would mean closing one's mind to the possible insight that the increase may have a *sociological explanation*. In reflective thinking, those who cast their nets wide are rewarded with the largest and most interesting catches.

INQUIRIES

The following inquiries are designed to provide exercise in reflective thinking. Your objective is to stimulate your sense of wonder and produce interesting lines of inquiry. Most of your journal entries should be in the form of questions. Any that are expressed as statements should be tentative rather than firm. (To make entries that close off inquiry rather than open it would, at this stage, be counterproductive.)

1. Review your responses to the Chapter 1 and 2 inquiries. Enter those responses in your journal.

2. Reread the discussions of Thomas Szasz, Viktor Frankl, Abraham Maslow, and Alfred Kinsey earlier in this chapter. Enter in your journal whatever questions come to mind about these discussions.

3. The chapter noted that "research reveals that the more often we hear an idea expressed, the more likely we are to accept it as true.... Research also reveals that most people will contradict the findings of their senses, at least on occasion, in order to gain the security of agreeing with others." List in your journal some popular ideas you have seldom, if ever, heard criticized. Be careful not to screen out

any. The ones that you are inclined to consider self-evident are the very ones that should be listed here. (Listing them does not constitute saying they are wrong. It merely focuses your attention on them. Worthy ideas will withstand examination.)

4. Extend the "Potpourri of Sample Questions" section by listing as many sociologically interesting questions as you can in your journal.

5. Review the chapter's discussion of the effects of TV violence. Reflect on the possible effects of other (that is, nonviolent) TV programming, such as game shows, the evening news, "tabloid" shows like *Hard Copy* and *A Current Affair*, talk shows, athletic events, and commercials. Reflect also on the possible effects of other communication and entertainment media—newspapers and magazines, radio, movies, and popular music. List your questions in your journal.

Note

1. Actually, Frankl's work predates Maslow's but was not introduced in the United States until the 1960s.

4

❧

Thinking Creatively

As was noted in Chapter 1, the thinking process has three stages. Reflective thinking is the ongoing phase in which curiosity is applied to observation and experience (including reading and listening) to discern interesting and worthwhile issues. When one of those issues is selected for closer examination, creative thinking and critical thinking are used to resolve it. The three kinds of thinking are distinguished mainly by the purposes for which they are used: reflective to *identify* issues, creative to *produce* ideas for resolving an issue, and critical to *evaluate* those ideas. They also differ in other ways. Creative thinking, for example, employs imaginativeness to a greater extent than reflective or critical thinking does. In addition, creative thinking is also divergent, seeking to gather all relevant evidence and all possible viewpoints and interpretations. Critical thinking, in contrast, is convergent, narrowing possibilities to probabilities and, where possible, probabilities to certainties.

These distinctions, although helpful in understanding and mastering the thinking process, should not be regarded as rigid. Asking questions is common to all three stages. Imaginativeness, a defining characteristic of creative thinking, may also be present in reflective or critical thinking. The order of stages in the thinking process may vary—for example, when a new perspective is conceived during the *critical* thinking stage. And critical thinking may be used independently of the other two kinds of thinking, notably when evaluating other people's ideas.

What Creative Thinking Entails

Thinking creatively involves clarifying the issue, accumulating the evidence necessary for a judgment to be made, and enumerating the possible interpretations and judgments that might be made about the evidence. Let's examine each of these considerations. (*Critical* thinking is discussed in Chapter 5.)

CLARIFYING THE ISSUE

Although it is an established practice to express issues as hypotheses, declarative statements tentatively setting forth a view of the issue which analysis will either prove or disprove, that practice often invites bias, particularly when used by novices. (A tentative assertion can easily harden into a belief and tempt us to gather evidence selectively, favoring whatever supports our hypothesis.) For this reason, it is preferable to express issues as *questions*. If you have used your journal effectively, you will have already recorded a variety of questions about the issue, and one of these may serve as the clearest and best expression. However, you may decide on a different expression. In either case, your aim should be to focus on precisely what it is you want to know.

Because the way an issue is expressed strongly influences the avenues of inquiry that are pursued and can even determine whether or not an insight is achieved, the task of clarifying the issue should be undertaken with care. Thoughtful consideration of a number of ways of expressing the issue will generally reward you with the most interesting, valuable expression. When most scholars researching gender were asking "Do men and women differ, and if so, who's better?" Carol Tavris (1992) asked "Why is everyone so interested in differences? Why are differences regarded as deficiencies? What functions does the *belief* in differences serve?" (p. 43). Those novel expressions led her to a number of uncommon and valuable insights, which she detailed in *The Mismeasure of Woman*.

Sometimes, your journal entry will be a cluster of questions, like the sample entry suggested in Chapter 3 about the explosion of the *DSM* classifications in recent years. After reviewing all these questions, you might decide that the essential issue is best expressed as "Why has the number of *DSM* classifications increased so dramatically since 1952?" This "clarified" expression of the issue would frame your subsequent investigation and analysis. (You would not, of course, necessarily ignore other questions. Each of them could be addressed at an appropriate time in the course of your investigation.)

ASSEMBLING THE EVIDENCE

To assemble evidence, first decide what kind of information will enable you to answer the issue as you have expressed it and then determine the source of that information. Because the answers to some questions will lie in unlikely places, and others will require you to do original research, you will need to be resourceful (hence the classification of assembling evidence as a *creative* thinking task). Arthur Schlesinger, Jr.'s (1993) analysis of multiculturalism was enhanced by an imaginative research strategy, which went beyond the current controversy and considered such historically related issues as assimilation, the "melting pot" concept, segregation, patriotism, and the civil rights movement. This approach led him to consult the works of distinguished black thinkers, past and present, including Frederick Douglass, W.E.B. Du Bois, Ralph Ellison, Richard Wright, Martin Luther King, Jr., William Raspberry, Orlando Patterson, John Hope Franklin, and Franklyn Jennifer.

Many researchers have wondered about to what extent, if any, viewing TV violence increases aggressiveness in children. The difficulty, of course, is to separate the influence of TV from other influences. One group of researchers took this ingenious approach: They compared three Canadian towns (whose names they disguised) almost identical in most respects, such as population and income, but different in one respect—accessibility to TV. One mountain town had had no television reception until 1974, the second had only the CBC (Canadian network TV), and the third had the CBC plus the three main U.S. networks, NBC, CBS, and ABC. After several years of research, they concluded,

> The finding that Notel children displayed more aggression 2 years after the introduction of television into their town further strengthens the evidence for a relationship between television and aggression demonstrated previously in laboratory, field, and naturalistic studies. Particularly striking about the results of this study is that the effects of television were not restricted to a subset of children. Boys and girls, children initially high and low in aggression, and those watching more or less TV were equally likely to show increased aggressive behavior. (Joy, Kimball, & Zabrack, 1988, pp. 153-154)

The most basic information sources, and the easiest to use, are the reference materials found in the library:

For facts and statistics: *World Almanac*, available from 1868; *Information Please Almanac; The New York Times Encyclopedic Almanac; Crime in the United States*, a U.S. Department of Justice compilation of relevant statistics; and *Statistical Abstracts of the United States*

For information about people: Among others, *Current Biography: Who's News and Why* and *Webster's Biographical Dictionary*

For information about the English language: Among others, *Oxford English Dictionary (OED), Webster's New Dictionary of Synonyms,* and Eric Partridge's *Dictionary of Slang and Unconventional English*

For information about articles: A complete list of indexes may be found in Eugene O. Sheehy's *Guide to Reference Books,* available in most libraries. Here is a brief listing of the indexes relevant to most sociological issues: *Social Science Index, Humanities Index* (before 1965 these two were combined and known as *International Index*), *New York Times Index, Education Index, United States Government Publications, Monthly Catalog, Applied Science and Technology Index,* and *Index to Legal Periodicals.*

For information about books: Your library's card/computer catalog

For general data retrieval: Today's technology has made it easier than ever to retrieve data. Numerous computer databases and abstracting services are available. Among the most relevant are *Sociological Abstracts, Psychological Abstracts, America: History and Life,* and *Dissertation Abstracts International.* Keep in mind that you needn't spend long, monotonous hours wading through irrelevant material. Just use tables of contents and indexes, flip to appropriate pages, and read only those pages.

If no relevant studies are available on the subject you are investigating, you will have to conduct your own research. The kinds of research methods most commonly employed by sociologists are described in the following sections:

Survey

A **survey** is a research instrument that employs questions to determine the opinions, beliefs, or behavior of a particular population (group of people). When the population is large, the survey is administered to a sample (a limited number of members of the group) rather than to the entire population. The survey is typically composed of fill-in or multiple-choice questions about the feelings, thoughts, or behaviors pertaining to the research issue. The survey may be mailed or delivered and self-administered, or it may be conducted in person or by telephone.

The sampling in a survey must be representative; that is, it must fairly represent the population being studied. This is usually achieved by a systematic approach, in which, for example, every 10th or 20th or 100th person on a list is contacted. There is no restriction on the size of the population studied—it may be as small as the residents of a dormitory or as large as the citizens of an entire country—as long as the results are expressed in terms of the population. To assume that the responses of a single dormitory on a single campus in a single state are representative of the entire country would, of course, be ludicrous. Survey questions must be carefully designed so as to be clear, unambiguous, and free of bias. If respondents cannot be sure what is being asked, or if the questions lead them to answer in support of the surveyor's bias, the survey's validity will be compromised.

Personal Interview

Related to the survey is the **personal interview** with someone who has expertise or firsthand experience in the area you are investigating. (Don't overlook the experts closest to you—the professors in your own institution.)

Observation

Observation, as the name implies, is watching an event or activity in person. The observer may stand apart from the action or be a participant in it. One example of participatory observation is living among a group of migrant workers in order to study their living conditions and relationships. Another is traveling with police officers on their duty tours to experience the conditions in which they work and the situations with which they must deal. Participatory observation is especially useful where the focus is on largely invisible effects such as attitudes and emotions. For example, Carol Rambo Ronai (1992) took a job as an erotic dancer to study the ways in which that occupation affects a woman's attitude toward self and others and her relationships with men.

Experiment

An **experiment** is a research initiative involving the manipulation of variables to determine their interrelationship. Researchers begin an experiment by forming one or more hypotheses—that is, statements whose truth or falsity can be demonstrated. Next, the researchers decide what the variables are and whether they are independent or controlled by other variables. (Variables are behavior characteristics that can be measured, rated, or scored.)

In a well-known experiment, Robert Rosenthal (1973) tested the hypothesis that classroom teachers' expectations affected students' academic performance; in other words, that students will tend to measure up or down to their teachers' opinion of their ability. Rosenthal administered an IQ test to all the children in a school. He then randomly chose certain students—*without looking at the test scores*—and informed their teachers that those students were unusually bright and could be expected to do especially well in their studies. When he returned 8 months later and administered another test, he found that the students he had arbitrarily designated as superior had outperformed the rest of the student body. The experiment had confirmed his hypothesis—the teachers' belief about those students had served as a self-fulfilling prophecy.

Experiments must be designed with care to rule out the possibility of hidden variables. Jeff Goldstein and Robert Arms (cited in Levin, 1993, pp. 38-39) interviewed fans before and after a football game to determine whether watching a violent sport increased their level of aggression, but then they realized that the type of person who attends football games could be predisposed to aggression or that the availability of alcohol at the games could lower inhibitions against aggressiveness. So they devised a more controlled experiment. College students in a psychology class were randomly selected to watch different kinds of sporting events—some, a swim meet; others, a hockey match; still others, professional wrestling. No alcohol was available for any event. The researchers found that aggressiveness increased with hockey and wrestling but not swimming.

Review of Published Data

A **review of published data** determines patterns or trends. To learn the extent to which hearsay influenced news, Jack Levin and Arnold Arluke (cited in Levin, 1993, p. 134) examined the front pages of the *New York Times* Sunday editions over a 12-month period and noted how many stories were unattributable to sources. They found that as many as 70% were.

Mixing Methods

A research study may employ a single method or a combination of two or more methods. For his study of the factors that produce excellence in athletic performance, Daniel E. Chambliss (1995) traveled with a successful swimming team as a participant observer. He lived with them and attended their meetings, training sessions, competitions, and social events. He also conducted interviews with swimmers, coaches, and officials. Finally, he incorporated his own (separate) experience as a swimming coach.

CONSIDERING ALL POSSIBLE INTERPRETATIONS AND JUDGMENTS

This part of the creative process is undoubtedly the most neglected, which explains the poverty of aspect observable in many novices in sociology and in most other academic disciplines. Even if these people manage to examine the evidence—and some don't even do that much, being content to assert a prefabricated opinion—they are in the habit of settling for the first response to the evidence that occurs to them, trusting that intuition will serve as well as rigorous thought. They fail to understand that the first response that occurs to any of us is likely to be a mindless playback of the most fashionable idea of the day, an idea that in all likelihood entered the memory by way of the ear rather than the mind and seems meritorious only because we have encountered it so often, not because we have compared it with other views and found it superior.

Wanting to reach closure efficiently and quickly is perfectly natural, but it is not consistent with excellence in thinking, so you must resist the tendency. If you rush to judgment, you are likely to confirm what you have always thought or what is in vogue. Although you will probably feel self-confident and wise as a result, you will nevertheless remain mired in whatever shallowness or error you may have fallen into by chance. The only way to avoid being victimized in this way is to *defer judgment until you have considered all major possibilities,* both those in fashion and those out of fashion, old as well as new. Take the time to consider all possibilities without prejudice, refusing to make any judgment until you have completed the following strategies and proceeded to the critical thinking phase.

1. **Brainstorm the issue.** Start with the basic pro and con view of the issue—"It is" versus "It isn't," "It does" versus "It doesn't," "It should" versus "It shouldn't." Then write down all the variations of those pro and con views that you have heard expressed about the issue. Don't screen any out, no matter how foolish they may have sounded at the time or how different they may be from your own view. Briefly note, as well, the evidence you have heard offered (or that might be offered) in support of the various views.

2. **Think of counterexamples.** According to the ancient Latin axiom *exceptio regulam probat*—"the exception *tests* the rule."[1] Thinking of counterexamples is therefore an especially helpful use of your imagination that will make the later task of critical thinking easier and more effective. Here's how to apply this strategy.[2] Look over the ideas you produced by brainstorming and the evidence that you've

heard offered in support of those ideas. Let's say you've written down the idea "people aren't influenced by what they see on TV or in movies." Try to think of as many examples as you can in which people have been influenced by something on the screen. One is the fact that an actor portraying a doctor on TV received 250,000 letters asking for medical advice, and another is that the depiction of fictional births, marriages, and deaths on soap operas often prompt viewers to send the characters cards and gifts (cited in Levin, 1995, pp. 36-37). Yet another example is the fact than when Michael Jordan began wearing baggy basketball shorts, no other player at any level of the sport wore them, yet within a few years, virtually *every* basketball player—in other words, millions of players in the United States and around the world—were wearing them.

3. **Play "devil's advocate" with the view that is most appealing to you.** This strategy, which is designed to help you resist the lure of the familiar, consists of taking a popular idea, one you're inclined to accept without question, and challenging it. Begin by stating the view that seems most reasonable to you and then reverse that view and list all the arguments and evidence that might be marshalled in support of the "reversed" view. The following three examples show this procedure in brief:

- **Example 1**

    Issue: The relationship between rock music and adolescent rebellion

    Your belief: Adolescent rebellion is responsible for the popularity of rock music.

    The reverse: The popularity of rock music is responsible for adolescent rebellion.

    Argument/evidence for the reverse: The lyrics of some rock music and the accompanying dramatizations in videos often convey the impression that teen rebellion is not only acceptable but expected behavior. They also suggest that teens know better than their parents and teachers what is best for them. These suggestions, particularly when made by entertainers whom teens tend to idolize, tend to encourage teen rebellion.

- **Example 2**

   Issue: The relationship between self-esteem and achievement

   Your belief: High self-esteem is positively correlated with achievement.

   The reverse: High self-esteem is negatively correlated with achievement.

   Argument/evidence for the reverse: In one study, American students boasted that they would score the highest on an examination and South Korean students predicted that they would score the lowest. The reverse occurred (cited in Weisman, 1991). A Purdue University study comparing problem-solving performances of high and low self-esteem groups concluded that "the higher the self-esteem, the poorer the performance" (McCormack, 1981, p. 10D).

- **Example 3**

   Issue: The effect of expressing one's anger

   Your belief: Expressing anger reduces anger.

   The reverse: Expressing anger increases anger.

   Argument/evidence for the reverse: After reviewing the research on the effects of expressing anger, Carol Tavris (1989) concluded,

   In study after study that I could find, [the] results are clear: talking can freeze a hostile disposition. . . . The cumulative effect of these studies supports good old-fashioned motherly advice: If you can't say something nice about a person, don't say anything at all—at least if you want your anger to dissipate and your associations to remain congenial. But if you want to stay angry, if you want to *use* your anger, keep talking. (pp. 134-135)

   4. **Construct relevant scenarios.** Think of a number of scenarios, preferably ones that (a) derive from your own experience or firsthand observation and (b) represent a variety of situations. (If you can't think of any real ones, hypothetical ones will do. Just be sure that they are plausible.) Record these scenarios in as much detail as you

can so that when you apply critical thinking you will be able to gauge how the idea or ideas in question fit those situations. Here are some sample scenarios you might construct if you were addressing the issue of whether expressing anger reduces it or increases it.

You are driving down the highway and someone cuts in front of you, almost causing an accident. Only your quick reaction of turning the wheel sharply while applying the brakes saves you. When fear gives way to anger, you give vent to your feelings, hoisting your hand in an obscene gesture and hurling epithets after the offender as he pulls away from you. Your foot joins in the condemnation by pressing harder on the gas pedal and you chase him (for precisely what purpose you have no idea). After racing behind him for a half-mile or so and employing maneuvers that make others gesture obscenely at you, you give up the chase but continue to voice your feelings to your passengers until you reach your destination a half-hour later. Then you proceed to tell the person you are visiting what happened, adding a final measure of vitriol, "I can't believe that *#@!! I hope he @!!/#!"

[Same situation, different reaction] After the driver cuts you off, and you feel anger rising in you, you decide to repress it so that it doesn't destroy the happy mood you have been enjoying. You make no gestures, utter no epithets, but instead turn to your traveling companions and say "Do you mind if I make a quick stop at my insurance agent's office? I'm thinking of increasing my coverage." Everyone laughs, albeit a little nervously.

At the monthly sales meeting, Arnold's boss announces her decision on who will be promoted to the position of district manager, which Arnold has sought. It will be a female coworker with less experience than Arnold. He is outraged and groans to the people on either side of him, "That beats everything. Talk about discrimination against women. This is discrimination by women against men." And that complaint is just for openers. Arnold continues the tirade after the meeting, during the carpool ride home, and that evening with his family. In fact, for the next week he seldom manages to think or speak of anything but his feelings of victimization and his contempt for the boss and the new district manager.

Getting the Most
From the Creative Process

Much of the effort of creative thinking consists of gathering and recording ideas that are not your own and in many cases directly oppose your own. If you are not accustomed to this activity, you may feel uncomfortable with it. "This is a waste of time," you may reason. "I already know the answer to the question, so there's no point in entertaining contradictory ideas." Or you may experience the vague feeling that by exploring other perspectives you are being disloyal to your own. Such feelings and thoughts are unreasonable and will block creativity if you do not resist them.

The value of exploring other ideas than your own lies in the fact that irony and paradox are alive and well and there is no reason to doubt their continued longevity. What seems indisputably insightful and wise may in time be found to be mistaken, and ideas that have been universally dismissed as ludicrous have occasionally proved meritorious. Even more to the point, the individuals who discover what others have missed are invariably people who have the intellectual humility to step away from their own ideas from time to time and show a measure of hospitality to unfamiliar and even foreign ideas.

INQUIRIES

Save your responses to the following inquiries. Chapter 5's inquiries will refer to them.

1. Chapter 3 mentioned the issue "Has child abuse increased over the past couple of decades, or is it just better reported now?" Decide how you would go about investigating this issue. Don't settle for the obvious approaches—apply your ingenuity. You don't have to do the research but do mention the specific sources you would use.

2. During the 1960s and 1970s, the idea of a "generation gap" received a lot of attention, and many regarded it as an inevitable, natural phenomenon. Some still do. But others wonder whether the tendency for American youths to challenge their parents' values is more a conditioned phenomenon than a natural one. (They speculate that publicity about it might have created a self-fulfilling prophecy.) Decide how you could test whether the generation gap is a natural phenomenon. Don't settle for the first few ideas that come to mind. Apply your creativity, develop a number of approaches, and explain them in detail.

3. Discuss how you would determine the attitudes of the members of your campus community on the subject of date rape. Begin by clarifying the issue, then explain what investigative approaches you would use and why. If you would use a survey, explain what questions you would ask.

4. Brainstorm each of the following ideas in the manner explained in the chapter:

   ■ The issue of whether the passive nature of television viewing has any impact on people's behavior—for example, whether it causes a loss of initiative, apathy toward voting, or gullibility.

   ■ The issue of whether capital punishment deters crime.

5. For each of the assertions listed below, think of a counterexample—that is, an actual case you know of that challenges the assertion:

   ■ Giving people something for nothing robs them of initiative.

   ■ Teenagers and young adults tend to look upon senior citizens with admiration and respect.

   ■ The current crop of Hollywood movies is relatively free of sex and violence.

6. Play "devil's advocate" with the following idea in the manner explained in the chapter:

   ■ Sex education classes help reduce promiscuity, teenage pregnancy, and the incidence of sexually transmitted diseases.

7. Psychologist Carl Rogers (1961), a pioneer in the development of humanistic psychology, said, "One of the basic things I was a long time in realizing, and which I am still learning, is that when an activity *feels* as though it is valuable or worth doing, it *is* worth doing" (p. 22). Construct at least five varied scenarios that will enable you to determine the reasonableness of this idea.

8. Select one of the following topics and list the various issues it calls to mind. Then apply the approach detailed in this chapter (i.e., clarify the issue, assemble the evidence, and consider all possible interpretations and judgments):

   ■ The possible influence of supermarket tabloids on people's ideals, aspirations, or worldviews

   ■ The claim made by some people that journalistic sensationalism has created a false view of contemporary life

   ■ The possible connection between the lyrics of heavy metal and/or rap music and violent crime, including rape

   ■ The possible connection between the media's emphasis on self-indulgence, impulsiveness, and instant gratification and contemporary social problems

   ■ The problems of academic deficiency and dropping out of school

9. Select an issue you recorded in your journal, one that derived from your own reflection rather than one presented in this book. Follow the directions given in Inquiry 8.

Notes

1. The popular reading "the exception *proves* the rule," which is nonsensical, is based on the erroneous rendering of *probat* as "proves" instead of "probes" (tests).

2. Be aware that although the strategy of counterexamples works very well with ideas that make assertions about *the way things are*—for example, "people appreciate what they earn more than what is merely given to them"—it does not work well with ideas that make assertions about *the way things should be*, such as a proposal for change. For the latter, other strategies are more effective.

5

❧

Thinking Critically

The most interesting and astounding contradiction in life is to me the constant insistence by nearly all people upon "logic," "logical reasoning," "sound reasoning," on the one hand, and on the other their inability to display it, and their unwillingness to accept it when displayed by others.

—Chester I. Barnard (1938, p. 303)

The accuracy of Barnard's point is readily observable in everyday experience. Why, then, do so few people acknowledge the insight and fewer still apply it in their intellectual lives? Because it's an unpleasant realization, and many people would prefer to pretend they are without fault. Anyone who would be a critical thinker, however, must get beyond this pretense. The best way to accomplish this is to focus more on rooting error out of *one's own* thinking than on detecting error in other people's thinking. Accordingly, although each of the strategies presented in this chapter may be used to evaluate other people's arguments, the emphasis throughout the chapter is on monitoring *your own* arguments. Maintaining this emphasis in the conduct of your intellectual affairs will not only help you become a better thinker—it will also improve your relationships with your associates. Although others may take offense if you shine the light of criticism too brightly on their ideas, no one will object if you do so on your own!

The most fundamental idea in critical thinking is the principle of contradiction: *A statement cannot be both true and false at the same time under the same circumstances.* Did O. J. Simpson kill Nicole Simpson and her companion? Either he did or he didn't. The possibility that he paid someone else to do so (an unlikely scenario) doesn't challenge the principle, for in that case he still would not have killed them himself. Do additional planets, as yet undiscovered, exist in our solar system? Have aliens visited this planet? If so, have they abducted people and subjected them to experiments on board their spacecrafts, as some popular books have alleged? Will nuclear war occur in your lifetime? Will a woman be elected president at any time during the next century? We may not yet know the answers to any of these questions; we may not *ever* know the answers to some of them. Nevertheless, in each case we can say with certainty that the answer cannot be both yes and no.[1]

The principle of contradiction keeps us mindful that ideas are seldom of equal quality—that solutions to problems range from the practical to the impractical, beliefs from well-founded to ill-founded, opinions from informed to uninformed, arguments from logical to illogical—and that only by conscientious research and analysis can we separate the more worthy from the less and, ultimately, identify the best. In short, the principle of contradiction is a spur to excellence in critical thinking.

A Strategy for Critical Thinking

Critical thinking complements creative thinking by evaluating the ideas produced in that phase. Creative thinking, as noted earlier, is divergent, widening our field of vision to encompass all possibilities. Critical thinking, however, is convergent, narrowing the possibilities first to probabilities and finally to the most reasonable choice, the view of the issue that is most defensible in light of the evidence. An effective strategy for critical thinking is to determine the most reasonable view, construct the argument for that view, and assess the logic of that argument.

DETERMINING THE
MOST REASONABLE VIEW

This first step consists of evaluating the ideas you generated in the creative thinking phase, using one of the following approaches:

1. **Consider the implications of the various responses to this issue.** When we endorse a viewpoint, logic usually requires us to endorse an entire network of ideas, some of which may not be immediately evident. Consider, for example, the idea advanced by extreme advocates of multiculturalism that African American studies should be taught only by African Americans. Arthur M. Schlesinger, Jr. (1993) noted an implication that exposes the shallowness of that idea: "The doctrine that only blacks can teach and write black history leads inexorably to the doctrine that blacks can teach and write only black history as well as to inescapable corollaries: Chinese must be restricted to Chinese history, women to women's history, and so on" (p. 105). Surely the advocates of multiculturalism do not intend that implication, yet it is a logically inescapable component of their idea. Schlesinger did not invent it; he only discovered it by careful analysis. (A more reasonable stipulation for multiculturalists to make would

be that only those who have the academic credentials to teach African American studies should be allowed to teach it. That would put the emphasis where it belongs, and it would not exclude any qualified person, regardless of his or her race.)

Here's how you might consider the implications of another important issue, namely, whether human beings have free will:

- The extreme "pro" idea: All human thoughts and actions are freely chosen by the individual. No outside forces—biological, social, or cultural—affect individual freedom.

  The implications: One is that our genes never affect our ability to choose, that low intelligence has little or no impact on the quality of decisions one makes. Another is that the circumstances of our lives do not limit the range of options open to us—an inner-city child is as free as a suburban child to resist the drug culture, attend an expensive prep school, and continue his or her education in a private college or university. A third implication is that the important people in our lives—parents, teachers, media role models— have no effect on our choices. Young girls whose dress and bearing mirror Madonna's were uninfluenced by Madonna; the many young men who wear earrings arrived at their decision to do so totally independent of current fashion.

- The extreme "con" idea: Free will is an illusion. All human thoughts and actions are determined by the individual's genetic endowment or sociocultural conditioning.

  The implications: Criminals should not be blamed for committing crimes because they could not have been at fault. People who do heroic deeds, such as risking their lives to save others, should not be praised because they had no choice in the matter but merely did what they were programmed to do. Self-help books and weight-loss programs that depend on will power are totally without merit. Scholarly debate is pointless because no one can ever decide to change his or her mind. Research and educational curriculums in problem solving, decision making, and creative/critical thinking are a waste of time and money. Books like this one are an exercise in futility.

Understanding the implications of an idea makes for a more informed choice about it (assuming that determinism is mistaken and choice is possible). In this case, you can say "I accept these implications" or "Given these implications, the idea must be unreasonable" and consider an alternative view. Fortunately, there is such a view, and its implications are quite compatible with everyday experience.

- The alternative idea: Free will is a reality, but it can be affected by a variety of factors, including heredity (more specifically, temperament) and the influences of home, school, church, and popular culture. In extreme conditions—for example, when a person is subjected to brainwashing techniques—free will may be seriously compromised. Nevertheless, people generally have the ability to overcome their conditioning.

  The implications: There are many gradations of free will. People's conditioning may create constraints on free will in certain matters but not in others. In most cases, it is reasonable to hold people responsible for their misdeeds and to praise them for their noble deeds. Scholarly debate and education for thinking can guide people in the exercise of their free will.

2. **Evaluate your counterexamples.** Decide how typical the examples that challenge your idea are. Chapter 4 listed the following counterexamples for the idea "people aren't influenced by what they see on TV or in movies": a TV doctor received 250,000 letters asking for medical advice; fictional births, marriages, and deaths on soap operas often prompt viewers to send the characters cards and gifts; and Michael Jordan started a fashion trend by wearing baggy shorts. After considering these and other examples, you would undoubtedly conclude that they are reasonably typical. Accordingly, you would reject the idea that people aren't influenced by what they see on television.

3. **Evaluate the ideas your "devil's advocacy" produced in the creative thinking phase.** Compare the original idea with its opposite and decide which is more reasonable. If you decide the original

one is, decide whether anything you considered for the other view suggests you should modify it. On the issues discussed in Chapter 4, you *might* decide as follows:

- Your initial belief that adolescent rebellion is responsible for the popularity of rock music is no more supportable than the view that the popularity of rock music is responsible for adolescent rebellion.
- Your initial belief that high self-esteem is positively correlated with achievement is not supported by the evidence. The opposite view is.
- Your initial belief that expressing anger reduces anger is not supported by the evidence. The opposite view is.

In many cases, of course, your initial belief will withstand criticism. But even in those cases, your "devil's advocacy" will have been useful in providing assurance of the reasonableness of your view.

4. **Appraise the scenarios you developed in your creative thinking.** Decide whether the effects would be favorable or unfavorable if the idea in question were implemented in these situations. If they would not be favorable, modify the idea accordingly.

5. **In light of your findings in Approaches 1 through 4, determine or construct the most reasonable view of the issue.** If one view proves correct and all others incorrect, adopt the correct one as your own, even if that means abandoning your initial view. Keep in mind, however, that even an erroneous view of an issue often contains a modest insight. Whenever that is the case, construct a new view of the issue that incorporates the insights of the conflicting views. Your final view of the adolescent rebellion/rock music issue, for example, might be this: *The popularity of rock music was created or at least enhanced by the spirit of rebelliousness in adolescents of the 1950s; since then, rock music has intensified that spirit by dramatizing and celebrating it.*

CONSTRUCTING YOUR ARGUMENT

An argument is composed of two or more premises (assertions) and a conclusion reasoned from those premises. In other words, an argument is a kind of verbal equation like $1 + 1 = 2$ or $2 - 1 = 1$. In fact, the words used to signal the different parts of the argument parallel the mathematical signs. In place of the plus sign, "and," "also," or "in addition," are used; in place of the minus sign, "but," "however," or "yet"; in place of the equal sign, "therefore," "so," or "consequently." (The choice of expressions in each case is, of course, greater than these examples illustrate.) Often, one of the premises in an argument is unexpressed. The person may be striving for brevity or simply be unaware of part of his or her argument. Because errors can occur in unexpressed premises as well as expressed ones, the missing premise(s) must be identified before the soundness of an argument can be determined. Look at the following examples:

- Standard expression

  All sociologists are mortal.

  Professor Rigor is a sociologist.

  Therefore, Professor Rigor is mortal.

- Argument with hidden premise

  Plea bargaining expedites the handling of court cases, so it is a valuable part of our judicial system.

  Comment. The full argument is as follows:

  Plea bargaining expedites the handling of court cases. Any procedure that expedites the handling of court cases is a valuable part of our judicial system. Therefore, plea bargaining is a valuable part of our judicial system.

  The hidden premise is untrue—not every procedure that expedites the handling of court cases is necessarily valuable. Therefore, the argument is flawed. (Note: Not every hidden premise will be flawed.)

Some arguments are complex; that is, they contain more than two premises and a conclusion. In some cases, they contain a series of interlocking premises and conclusions. (They may also contain hidden premises.)

- Complex argument

  Whatever is given the media spotlight is, in a sense, glamorized. More and more in recent years, behavior that used to be considered bizarre or unseemly is being given the media spotlight on the talk shows—for example, 40-year-olds dating teenagers and fathers and sons who date the same women. Therefore, bizarre and/or unseemly behavior is in a sense being glamorized. Moreover, young people and impressionable adults tend to emulate whatever is glamorized in the media. Therefore, behavior that used to be considered bizarre or unseemly is in all likelihood being emulated by young people and impressionable adults.

ASSESSING YOUR ARGUMENT

Assessing your argument means examining it for violations of logic, the various ways that thinking can go awry in constructing arguments. (Everyone, remember, no matter how elevated his or her status as an expert, is susceptible to error.) A close study of formal logic is beyond the scope of this book. It is enough to consider how to distinguish a sound argument from an unsound one. For an argument to be sound, the premises must be true and the conclusion must follow inescapably from them—in other words, no other conclusion can be logically possible.

The errors that occur in constructing an argument may be broadly classified under two headings: defective premise and defective conclusion.

DEFECTIVE PREMISE

If the premise is defective, the argument is tainted. Here are the most common errors that occur in a premise.

Misstatement of fact. This error is arguably the most common one and should be the first one you check for. When a curriculum revision group charged that monocultural Eurocentric bias was damaging to minority children, one analyst effectively challenged the accuracy of the very notion of monocultural Eurocentric bias. He wrote,

> The idea that Europe has produced one homogeneous culture seems rather weird. What is so "monocultural" about the wild mix of people from Reykjavik to Athens and from Lisbon to Omsk? Can Henry Adams and the person he once described as "a snarling Yacoob or Ysaac still reeking of the Ghetto, snarling a weird Yiddish to the officers of the customs" be usefully regarded as products of a single culture? Churchill and Hitler, St. Francis and Machiavelli, Pericles and Dracula—monocultural? (Schlesinger, 1993, p. 88)

Overgeneralization. A generalization is a judgment made about a class of people or things based on observation of a number of members of that class. Overgeneralization is a generalization based on insufficient observation. It takes for granted that the individuals observed are necessarily typical of the larger group, thus ignoring the possibility of individual differences. To avoid overgeneralization, be sure your judgments are scaled to fit your data.

Oversimplification. Simplification is acceptable, even necessary. Experts in any field simplify whenever they present complex ideas to laypeople. Teachers of young children also do so. The difference between simplification and oversimplification is that the latter doesn't merely make an idea easy to understand—it distorts it.

Whenever the issue you are dealing with is complex, take special care that your assertions reflect that complexity.

False cause. The most common error of false cause is known in logic as the post hoc fallacy, after the Latin *post hoc ergo propter hoc*— "after this, therefore because of this." In actuality, however, one event may follow another without being caused by the other, so you must never assume that any juxtaposition in time is sufficient to account for causation—you need additional evidence.

False analogy. There is an old saying in logic that "every analogy limps"; in other words, the most accurate and incisive analogy never represents the situation perfectly because, by definition, analogy is an attempt to explain one thing in terms of another very different thing. This does not mean that analogy should be avoided, only that it should be used with care and never be made to bear the burden of an argument.

A good example of the persuasive power of an effective analogy occurred in a letter published in the *Wall Street Journal* criticizing the standard line that if parents don't like TV fare they should "just switch channels." The author compared that advice to dealing with water pollution by advising people not to drink the water, air pollution by telling them not to breathe the air, and garbage in the streets by counseling them not to use the streets (cited in Feder, 1993, pp. 146-147). Logical purists would, of course, expect the author to make the case that television fare is reasonably classified as a form of pollution.

Failure to note distinctions. This kind of error confuses things that should be kept separate. The main forms it takes and the reasons for avoiding them are as follows:

- The person is distinct from his or her idea; therefore, attacks on the person should never be used as a substitute for analysis of an idea.

- Familiarity is not the same as validity, so the level of comfort you feel with an idea should never be taken for a measure of the idea's quality.
- Matters of judgment are distinct from matters of preference. Although preferences require no justification, judgments should be based on sufficient evidence, carefully weighed.

Unwarranted assumptions. Assumptions are ideas that are taken for granted. They may be warranted (justified) or unwarranted. Unwarranted assumptions are formed arbitrarily in matters where there is reasonable ground for disagreement. Because assumptions are usually implied but not expressed, they can affect our thinking without our awareness. Here are some common ones:

People's senses are always trustworthy. (Comment: Beliefs and desires can distort perception, causing us to see and hear selectively or inaccurately.)

Having reasons proves that one has reasoned logically. (Comment: Reasons may be borrowed uncritically from others, and even if they have been reasoned out, they may be illogical rather than logical.)

Conviction constitutes proof. (Comment: It is possible to be passionately committed to an error.)

Familiar ideas are more valid than unfamiliar ideas. (Comment: Familiarity merely indicates having heard or read the idea before; it provides no guarantee that what we heard or read was correct.)

If one event follows another in time, it must have been caused by the other. (Comment: The closeness in time could have been accidental.)

If the majority believes something, it must be correct. (Comment: Majorities have been wrong—for example, in supporting the execution of witches and in condoning slavery.)

The way things are is the way they should be. (Comment: Humans are imperfect and their inventions, including ideas, often need improving.)

The either/or fallacy. This error may be classified as an assumption, but it is important enough to warrant its own category. The either/or fallacy is the assumption that the only views that merit consideration are extreme views. Many contemporary controversies are presented in either/or terms: the theory of evolution versus creationism, nurture versus nature, censorship versus totally unrestricted expression of ideas, and liberalism versus conservatism, to name but a few. To avoid the either/or fallacy, ask "Are my choices really limited to one extreme view or the other? Is there no other alternative to those views?" If there is an alternative, an idea that accepts part of both extreme views or one that rejects both in their entirety, give it careful consideration.

DEFECTIVE CONCLUSION

A conclusion may be defective in either of two situations. The first is where the evidence supporting it is insufficient both in quantity and kind to permit that judgment to be made. Let's say you have examined a number of widely publicized arguments offered against abortion and noted that they all reflect a religious perspective, so you draw the conclusion that *the pro-life position on abortion is founded exclusively on religious belief and has no basis in law.* Even though you would have considerable company in that view, the conclusion is defective. The quantity of your evidence may or may not have been sufficient, but the *kind* was too narrow to permit a judgment to be made about the pro-life position's lack of any "basis in law." Before you could make that determination, you'd at least have to search the relevant law literature.

As explained in Chapter 2 (pp. 28-29), such a search would prove your conclusion to be not merely technically defective but thoroughly mistaken. Since 1975, the Constitutional Court of Germany has held the exactly opposite legal view—that "the life of each individual human being is self-evidently a central value of the legal order . . . [and] the constitutional duty to protect this life also includes its preliminary stages before birth." The German high court reaffirmed this view in 1993, holding that "the State has a duty to place itself protectively before unborn human life, shielding this life from unlawful attacks" and calling for penal laws against anyone who would pressure pregnant women into having abortions (cited in Arkes, 1994, p. 16).

You would then have to revise your conclusion, acknowledging that the pro-life position has a basis in law but that either U.S. scholars have failed to articulate that basis or the media have neglected to report scholarly arguments accurately.

The second situation in which a conclusion may be defective is in the case where it does not follow logically from the premises. Here the evidence may be sufficient both in quantity and kind, but the reasoning is deficient. To clarify this, look at some examples of logical and illogical reasoning.

- LOGICAL reasoning

    All sociologists are mortal.

    Professor Rigor is a sociologist.

    Therefore, Professor Rigor is mortal.

    Comment: This example, mentioned earlier in this chapter to illustrate the standard expression of an argument (known in logic as a syllogism), exhibits logical reasoning because the conclusion follows inescapably from the assertions (premises)—the professor is one of a group of people, all of whom are mortal, so he too must be mortal.

Judging the quality of reasoning in an argument is different from judging the truth of the assertions in the argument (or the truth of the conclusion, which, of course, is also an assertion). To illustrate this distinction, let's change the argument to

    All sociologists are infallible.

    Professor Rigor is a sociologist.

    Professor Rigor is infallible.

This argument is unsound but not because the reasoning is flawed; indeed, the reasoning is technically logical. The argument is unsound for a different reason—the first assertion is false. (The conclusion, considered as an assertion, is thus also false.)

- ILLOGICAL reasoning

  Example 1

  Sociologists are social scientists.

  Psychologists are social scientists.

  Therefore, all sociologists are psychologists.

  Comment: Both the premises are true—sociologists and psychologists are social scientists. But two groups can fit into the same general classification without being identical in every respect. (Note: The universal term "all" is sometimes expressed and sometimes omitted. The rule that logicians follow is any assertion that does not contain a qualifying phrase such as *some, many, the sociologists of the 19th century* and so on should be considered a universal. Thus, the two premises in this case should be considered to imply "all.")

  Example 2

  All students must obey campus regulations.

  No faculty are students.

  Therefore, no faculty must obey campus regulations.

  Comment: Obeying campus regulations is a requirement of being a student, but they are not the only ones who must meet that requirement. Faculty, staff, and administrators must, too. So the fact that faculty are not students has no bearing on the applicability of the requirement to them.

  Example 3

  All legitimate welfare recipients are in need of financial assistance.

  Some inner-city residents are legitimate welfare recipients.

  Therefore, all inner-city residents are in need of financial assistance.

  Comment: The "some" referred to in the second premise leaves many individuals unaccounted for, and those individuals may be poor, middle class, or wealthy. So it is illogical to conclude that "all" of them need financial assistance.

Reasoning may also take a hypothetical ("if . . . then") form, which may be logical or illogical. Here are some examples of each form:

- LOGICAL hypothetical form

    If sociologists are capable of error, students should not accept their views unquestioningly.

    Sociologists are capable of error.

    Therefore, students should not accept their views unquestioningly.

- ILLOGICAL hypothetical form

    Example 1

    Whenever I have applied myself conscientiously in a course, I have gotten a good grade.

    I got a good grade in this course.

    Therefore, I applied myself conscientiously in this course.

    Comment: The first premise doesn't say that conscientious application is the only way to get a good grade. It just says that it's one way. The possibility is open for others to exist—an understanding professor, for example.

    Example 2

    If the Board of Directors attend the meeting, the district supervisors attend.

    The Board of Directors did not attend the meeting.

    Therefore, the district supervisors did not attend the meeting.

    Comment: The first premise asserts only that the district supervisors attend whenever the Board of Directors attend. It leaves open the possibility that the district supervisors also attend at other times. (Unlike the Board of Directors, they may be required to attend all meetings.)

    Example 3

    If I win the lottery I'll pay all my bills.

    Therefore, if I pay all my bills I'll win the lottery.

Comment: The premise asserts that if an event outside my control occurs, I will perform an action that is within my power to perform. It does not logically follow that by performing said action, that which is outside my control will (magically) become controllable.

Example 4

If researchers ignore important items of evidence, they will err in their conclusions.

Therefore, if researchers do not ignore important items of evidence they will not err in their conclusions.

Comment: In saying that ignoring evidence leads to error, the premise does not rule out the possibility of other paths to error, such as misinterpreting. Accordingly, researchers may commit errors even on occasions in which they pay close attention to all the evidence.

Used with care, hypothetical reasoning is especially helpful in situations where two or more alternative possibilities exist and you wish your judgment to cover both (all) of them. Here, for example, is how one researcher expressed his view of the death penalty:

If the alternative in response to a brutal, hideous murder is life imprisonment with parole eligibility, then I am indeed in favor of the death penalty. If, however, the alternative is a life sentence without the possibility of ever being paroled, then capital punishment becomes unnecessary for the protection of society and I am therefore against it. (Levin, 1993, pp. 79-80)

INQUIRIES

1. Select one of the two issues you brainstormed in Inquiry 4 of Chapter 4 (the issue of television viewing's impact on people's behavior or the issue of whether capital punishment deters crime). Then apply critical thinking to the ideas you produced, using the approach explained in this chapter. That is, first determine the most reason-

able view by considering the implications of the various responses to the issue and then construct and assess your argument.

2. Select one of the three issues for which you selected a counterexample in Inquiry 5 of Chapter 4 (giving people something for nothing robs them of initiative; teenagers and young adults tend to look upon senior citizens with admiration and respect; and the current crop of Hollywood movies is relatively free of sex and violence). Decide whether that counterexample you produced for Inquiry 5 is typical or untypical. (If you aren't sure, consider additional examples that support or challenge the idea and then make your decision.) Finally, determine the most reasonable view of the issue and then construct and assess your argument on the issue, as explained in this chapter.

3. Appraise the scenarios you produced in response to the Carl Rogers quotation in Inquiry 7 of Chapter 4. Then determine the most reasonable view of the issue and construct and assess your argument on the issue.

4. Select one of the issues you analyzed in Inquiry 8 or 9 of Chapter 4. Then apply all appropriate critical thinking approaches, as detailed in this chapter, determine the most reasonable view, and construct and assess your argument.

Note

1. Certain kinds of questions are best answered "yes AND no"—for example, "Do prison rehabilitation programs prevent recidivism among child molesters?" The answer is that *some* programs succeed with *some* child molesters. But such cases do not challenge the principle of contradiction because the circumstances involved are different. (In other words, the same rehabilitation programs do not succeed and fail at the same time in the same way for the same individuals.)

6

❧

Making Ethical Decisions

Considerable confusion exists about ethics in contemporary Western society. Some philosophers have claimed that it is impossible to get from an *is* to an *ought;* in other words, that no amount of knowledge of how people *actually do* behave is sufficient to provide a basis for determining how they *should* behave. Thus, they have argued that ethics can only be a descriptive discipline, not a normative one (one that sets norms for behavior). The logical extension of this view is that decisions about right and wrong are entirely subjective and personal, so no individual group, or society is justified in setting moral standards and expecting others to conform to them. This view dominates popular culture and is often expressed on television and in popular books and magazines in constructions like these:

- Whatever an individual believes is morally right *is* morally right for that individual.

- Morality is relative.
- In matters of ethics I have a right to my opinion.
- It's wrong to make value judgments.

In many circles, challenging another's moral reasoning is considered the height of bad manners.[1]

Although it may seem enlightened at first consideration, this view of ethics does not bear scrutiny very well and sociologists have a special reason for understanding its deficiencies—because ethical considerations are prominent both in their professional relationships and in the relationships of the men and women whose interactions with social agencies they study.

The idea that it is impossible to get from an *is* to an *ought* contradicts a central fact of life—that every day each of us is faced with significant choices we cannot avoid making. Do we go to work or call in sick? Follow the research protocol or violate it? Put quotes around borrowed phrasing or leave them off, pretending the words are our own? Answer a colleague's question truthfully or lie? Stop for the red light or go through it? Pay our bills or spend the money on entertainment instead? In such cases, we may be free to respond as we choose, but we are not free to avoid responding. And our response says something more than "This is what I am doing because this is what I am doing." It says "I consider the choice I made preferable to the one I didn't make." Regardless of how we define "preferable" in any particular case (less troublesome, more enjoyable, in our interest, or some other way), the underlying assumption is the same—that we *ought* to do what is preferable.

Thus, *ought* is deeply embedded in all our significant choices. Whether we accept or reject the idea that it is impossible to proceed from *is* to *ought*, the fact remains that it is perfectly natural to do so. Daily life requires it. The effect of the philosophical doctrine that we can't do so has not been to elevate ethical discourse but to devalue it by denying ethical judgment an objective basis and regarding all choices as equally informed. In this way, the distinction between right and wrong behavior has been undermined and the entire lexicon of ethics has been rendered meaningless. Unfortunately, although the traditional standard of ethical judgment has been dismantled, the need for such a standard has remained constant. The legal system is no substitute for ethics because ethics guides law rather than the reverse. Before laws can be formulated, legislators must decide what to protect, what to proscribe, and why. The only way to make such determinations is by moral reasoning, the consideration of what *ought* to be protected or proscribed.

Corporations and communities of scholars also need standards to ensure that their internal and external relationships meet the requirements of ethics. Virtually every sizable organization has a carefully framed code of ethics. The American Sociological Association (ASA) is no exception. Its code, published in 1989, sets guidelines for the practice of sociology, publications and review process, teaching and supervision, and ethical obligations of employers, employees, and sponsors.[2] It also sets forth in detail the policies and procedures of its Committee on Professional Ethics. The preamble of this code attests to the importance of ethics in the discipline:

> Sociologists recognize that the discovery, creation, transmission, and accumulation of knowledge and the practice of sociology are social processes involving ethical considerations and behavior at every stage. Careful attention to the ethical dimensions of sociological practice, teaching, and scholarship contributes to the broader project of finding ways to maximize the beneficial effects that sociology may bring to humankind and to minimize the harm that might be a consequence of sociological work. . . . [T]he Code is meant to sensitize all sociologists to the ethical issues that may arise in their work, and to encourage sociologists to educate themselves and their colleagues to behave ethically.

Insufficient Bases of Ethical Judgment

In the confusion that has surrounded the subject of ethics for most of the 20th century, the basis of ethical judgment has been variously defined as personal feelings, the individual conscience, and the majority view. All three definitions have serious defects. Feelings has become the most fashionable of the three because the entertainment media tend to celebrate it more than the others, but it is hardly a new idea. In his well-known *Emile,* French philosopher Jean-Jacques Rousseau (1712-1778) wrote that all that he felt was right was right and that whatever he felt was wrong was wrong. The contemporary notion is similar—impulses and urges are unerringly correct and should therefore be followed unquestioningly. The problem is that everyday experience contradicts this assessment no less today than it did 200 years ago. Following the urge to cut classes or avoid studying can lead to failure in a course and even, if repeated often enough, to dismissal from college. Giving in to the urge to "push the pedal to the metal" and see how fast the car will go can lead to a date in traffic court or a slab in the morgue.

The experience of most of the convicts that crowd the nation's prisons offers eloquent testimony to the inadequacy of feelings as a basis of ethical judgment—the feelings they followed in stealing, assaulting, raping, and murdering, far from guiding them reliably, victimized them. Do feelings always lead people astray? Not at all. On some occasions, they prompt admirable behavior. The point is that it's foolish to place blind faith in feelings. Instead of trusting them implicitly we need to analyze them and determine their merit.

Individual conscience—our sense of right and wrong, the inner "voice" that says yes or no to actions—is a more reasonable standard of judgment than feelings. If carefully developed, it can guide us dependably and well, providing awareness of situations requiring moral choice and a sense of proportion in addressing those situations. The problem is that developing one's conscience is a difficult task, especially in a society that assigns little value to moral sensitivity. It is much easier and more comfortable to follow feelings and pretend that one is obeying the dictates of conscience. The fact that many people feel no compunction about treating others uncivilly and some criminals apparently feel no remorse even after committing heinous crimes suggests that the easier path is also a popular one.

The third common basis for making ethical decisions is the majority view. This basis has been reinforced by cultural relativism, the notion that whatever a culture decides is right is right for that culture. On occasion, however, the majority in every culture has been wrong. In ancient times, infanticide enjoyed majority support as did the sacrifice of young women to ensure a good harvest. In our own time, majorities have endorsed genocide and unspeakable violence against women; indeed, in some societies these outrages still exist. And in our own culture it took more than 100 years after the abolition of slavery (in its time a majority-approved institution) for government-sponsored racial discrimination to be overcome. The fact that a majority holds a particular view offers no assurance that the view is morally valid.

These three popular bases of ethical judgment are not only mistaken, they commit essentially the same mistake—assuming that people are infallible (incapable of error). The basis of feelings and that of conscience assume individual infallibility; the majority view, group infallibility. Accordingly, a more reliable basis of moral judgment is needed.

A Sound Basis for Moral Judgment

To say that it is possible to get from an *is* to an *ought* does not mean that the journey is without difficulty. Making ethical decisions involves the same processes as any other thinking challenge: thinking reflectively to identify moral issues and then thinking creatively and critically in an effort to find the most informed and reasonable response to those issues. Yet the challenge in ethical reasoning differs in one respect from other reasoning: It measures ideas not only against the standard of logic but also against that of ethics. Making ethical decisions requires familiarity with ethical principles and criteria and meticulousness in applying them to issues.

THE FUNDAMENTAL PRINCIPLE:
RESPECT FOR PERSONS

The principle of respect for persons is acknowledged in virtually all ethical systems. It is composed of three requirements, which Errol E. Harris (1969) explains as follows:

> First, that each and every person should be regarded as worthy of sympathetic consideration, and should be so treated; secondly, that no person should be regarded by another as a mere possession, or used as a mere instrument, or treated as a mere obstacle, to another's satisfaction; and thirdly, that persons are not and ought never to be treated in any circumstances as mere expendables. (p. 113)

This principle needn't be accepted on faith. It may—indeed, *should*—be tested in the manner set forth in Chapters 4 and 5: by examining its implications, by considering counterexamples, by playing "devil's advocate" and challenging it, and by conceiving and appraising scenarios in which it would apply.[3] The main implications of the principle of respect for persons are that a single standard should be applied in the treatment of individuals, that every person possesses a dignity that may not in any circumstances be ignored, that no one has the right to use other people as if they were things, and that this demanding standard of treatment is required even if one's feelings, one's conscience, or the majority endorses a lesser standard. (These implications, interestingly, are consistent with the "unalienable rights" spoken of in the Declaration of Independence.)

Because the principle of respect for persons is expressed in *should* form, the strategy of counterexamples is not applicable (see the explanation in Chapter 4). "Devil's advocate" and scenarios, however, are applicable. Playing "devil's advocate" involves reversing the principle in this manner—*No* person should be regarded as worthy of sympathetic consideration; *any* person may be regarded by another as a mere possession, used as a mere instrument, or treated as a mere obstacle to another's satisfaction; persons *ought to be treated* as mere expendables—and then considering the evidence that might be offered in support of this view. (If you find it impossible to conceive of any evidence that could reasonably be offered in support of this view, you will be in the company of the majority of ethicists in most ethical traditions.)

The kinds of scenarios in which the principle of respect for persons is relevant are many and varied. Here are just a few:

- Example 1

   Three people apply for a new position in a company. The executive responsible for making the hiring decision realizes that one of the candidates is a member of his fraternal lodge. He is inclined to award the position to that person without seriously considering the others.

- Example 2

   A graduate school professor is submitting a paper for which the bulk of the research, including the analysis of data, was done by two doctoral students under her supervision. The professor must choose whether to list as author herself only or the doctoral students and herself; also, if she chooses the latter, she must decide whether her name or theirs will be placed first.

- Example 3

   A husband and wife both hold professional positions, although in different fields. The husband has been offered a position in a distant city in which the likelihood is slim that his wife will be able to find a suitable position. He is assuming she will accompany him.

The question you would address is whether the principle of respect for persons is an important (although not necessarily the only) consideration in these cases. If you decide it is so, and moreover find that you are unable to conceive of a scenario that challenges the reasonableness of the principle, you may conclude that it is valid.

THE JUDGMENT CRITERIA

From the principle of respect for persons, three criteria of ethical judgment may be derived. Our relationships with other people create *obligations* of various kinds—notably parental, spousal, civic, and professional ones. In the fulfillment of these obligations, we are guided by *ideals*, and consideration of the *consequences* of different responses can help us identify the good or harm that each will produce. Let's look more closely at each of the criteria, particularly as they relate to decision making in sociology.

Obligations

The most obvious kind of obligation is a formal agreement with specific behavioral requirements clearly spelled out. (Such an agreement usually has legal as well as moral force.) Many other obligations, some considerably less formal, also exist. Friendship creates an obligation to keep confidences, be supportive in times of need, and honor the relationship by refusing to indulge in backbiting. Business obligations make demands on both employers and employees: The former have a moral duty to pay wages that are consistent with the demands of the work and the level of performance, the latter have an obligation to perform their duties diligently, and both have an obligation to deal with customers or clients honestly and conscientiously, providing quality products and/or services.

Membership in a profession entails special ethical obligations. Lawyers must serve the interests of their clients; doctors must do their best to maintain or restore the good health of their patients.

Among the obligations found in the ASA *Code of Ethics* are the following:

> Sociologists should strive to maintain objectivity and integrity in the conduct of sociological research and practice.

> Sociologists should not misuse their positions as professional social scientists for fraudulent purposes or as a pretext for gathering intelligence for any organization or government.

> An editor's commitment to publish an essay [in a sociological journal] must be binding on the journal.

> Sociologists must refrain from exploiting students.

> Sociologists must acknowledge all persons who contribute to their research and to their copyrighted publications. Claims and ordering of authorship and acknowledgments must accurately reflect the contributions of all main participants in the research and writing process, including students, except in those cases where such ordering or acknowledgment is determined by an official protocol. [Note that this statement bears directly on the scenario about the graduate school professor mentioned in example 2 on page 95.]

Like any other sociological conclusions, the *Code of Ethics* is subject to reevaluation whenever questions arise about one or another of its provisions. The case of James Richard Scarce is illustrative. Scarce, a doctoral candidate in sociology, was conducting a study of the radical environmental movement when questions arose about possible criminal vandalism committed by movement members. A federal district court ordered Scarce to testify about conversations he had had with one of the men alleged to have been involved in the crime. Scarce refused to testify, claiming his professional code of ethics as a sociologist required him to regard the conversations as confidential and privileged. Because the law acknowledges as privileged only communications with spouses, physicians, lawyers, the clergy, and (to a limited extent) journalists, Scarce was held in contempt of court and eventually spent 159 days in jail.

This case has sparked debate of the following statement in the *Code of Ethics*, which was the basis of Scarce's refusal to testify: "Confidential information provided by research participants must be treated as such by sociologists, *even when this information enjoys no legal protection or privilege and legal force is applied*" (emphasis added). One scholar, attorney and professor of public affairs Murray Comarow (1993), has pointed out that the ethical codes of several other social science associations take a different view of the ethical requirements of such situations. The American Political Science Association, he notes, emphasizes the importance of confidentiality but adds that scholars should "exercise appropriate restraint in making claims as to the confidential nature of their sources, and resolve all reasonable doubts in favor of full disclosure" (p. A44). The American Anthropological Association and the American Psychological Association take similar views, Comarow found. The debate could eventually result in the revision of the American Sociological Association's regulation on disclosure.

Ideals

Ideals are notions of excellence that clarify and reinforce obligations. Perhaps the most fundamental ideal is the Golden Rule—"Do unto others as you would have them do unto you." Other important ideals that are relevant to the ethical issues that sociologists deal with are fairness, justice, loyalty, tolerance, compassion, amity, love, and peace.

Consequences

The axiom that actions have consequences is supported by everyday experience. Even the smallest of deeds has some effect on those it touches, including the person who commits it. Some consequences

are physical; others are intellectual or emotional. Some occur immediately; others only with the passing of time. Some are intended;
others are unintended. Some are obvious; others are subtle and disguised by appearances. When the action in question has taken place
in the distant past, it may be possible to identify its consequences
with certainty. However, when the action has not yet been taken, when
the analysis is undertaken to determine which of several courses of
action is most ethical and therefore should be taken, we can only
speculate about what effects are likely to follow. Still, if approached
thoughtfully, such speculation can draw upon knowledge of parallel
situations whose consequences have been established.

Complicating the consideration of consequences is the fact that
they are often of mixed character. The same action that benefits one
person may harm others, or the effects may be entirely favorable at
the time the action is completed but unfavorable at some future time.
But the most difficult situation, from the standpoint of analysis, is
that in which the action produces some good and some bad effects
for everyone involved—both now and in the future. For this reason,
your assessment of consequences should never be casual, cursory, or
conducted in such a way as to approve what you want to do (or in
past situations, actually did). Only by accounting for all the actual or
probable effects will you be in a position to judge fairly and wisely.

THREE SUPPLEMENTARY PRINCIPLES

Three supplementary principles are helpful when applying the
three judgment criteria, for reasons that will be explained. The principles are as follows:

The principle of priorities. If two or more obligations exist, they
may be in conflict. The same is true of two or more ideals. Also, an
ideal may conflict with an obligation. In such cases, honoring one
will necessitate violating the others. Such a conflict existed for James
Richard Scarce. Civic duty demanded that he testify, whereas the

obligation created by the ASA *Code of Ethics* required him to maintain silence. The dilemma that confronted him was which course to choose. The principle of priorities—*when obligations and/or ideals conflict, determine which deserves priority*—undoubtedly guided his judgment. Of course, it is possible to apply this principle and choose unwisely.[4] Accordingly, it is important not merely to assign priorities but to be able to support them with sound reasoning.

The principle of greater good/lesser evil. Occasionally, either all the choices of action will be good or all will be evil. When all are good, this principle directs us to choose the one that represents the *greater* good. Similarly, when all possible choices are evil, this principle directs us to choose the one that represents the *lesser* evil.

The principle that circumstances can alter cases. This principle should not be confused with moral relativism. Moral relativism asserts that the moral quality of an act depends on individual perspective—if I view an act as permissible, then it is so for me, and if you view the same act as morally wrong, then it is wrong for you. That viewpoint implicitly denies the principle of respect for persons and diminishes the importance of the criteria of judgment. In contrast, the principle that circumstances can alter cases asserts that the moral quality of an act *depends on the character of the act itself* and this can be subtly altered by the circumstances of the case. In other words, this principle says that the character of an act is not affected by anyone's perspective or feelings or preferences.

This principle is the basis for many distinctions in the law, notably the distinction between first degree murder, second degree murder, manslaughter, and justifiable homicide. Just as a prosecuting attorney must study the details of the case to know its true nature, an ethicist must know the circumstances before making a moral judgment.

Making Moral Decisions: A Strategy

Knowing ethical principles and judgment criteria is one thing; being able to apply them to actual issues is quite another. The following approach will help you do so efficiently, effectively, and confidently. Use it whenever you are confronted with a moral issue—that is, an issue that involves a question of right and wrong, an issue in which respect for persons is a consideration. (Remember, the principle of respect for persons applies to you as well as to others.) Review the following criteria and ethical principles (indicated in boldface):

1. Decide what **obligations,** if any, are present.
2. Decide what moral **ideals,** if any, are relevant.
3. If obligations conflict with one another, or with ideals, determine which deserves the highest **priority** and why.
4. Determine what courses of action are open (be ingenious) and the **consequences** of each (be thorough).
5. In light of the **circumstances** of the case, decide what the most moral action would be. If your only choice is between two goods, choose the **greater good;** if it is between two evils, choose the **lesser evil.** Check your reasoning to be sure it is free of all the errors of logic described in Chapter 5.

INQUIRIES

1. List as many moral issues as you can think of that are of sociological interest. (A moral issue, remember, is an issue involving a question of right or wrong behavior.)
2. Select a moral issue from the list you prepared in Inquiry 1. Then apply the five-step strategy presented at the end of this chapter.

Notes

1. In contemporary usage in general and as used here specifically, the terms "ethical" and "moral" are interchangeable. A distinction may be made in the way the terms are used—the academic discipline, for example, is always ethics and never morality—but it is essentially a distinction without a real difference.

2. Because of the American Sociological Association's code's conciseness (only eight pages), quotations from it are given without specific page citations.

3. Because of space limitations, this chapter's discussion of how these strategies would apply to the principle of respect for persons is not as detailed as yours would be.

4. In Scarce's case, one might argue that the civic obligation deserved priority because the *Code of Ethics* directive was flawed and therefore not morally binding but that Scarce incurred no moral blame because he presumably acted in good faith.

7

❧

Constructing a
Persuasive Argument

In Chapter 5, you saw that an argument is essentially an equation
that is expressed in words rather than numbers and that the different
parts of an argument parallel the signs used in a mathematical equation (e.g., in place of the plus sign, "and," "also," or "in addition" is
used; in place of the minus sign, "but," "however," or "yet"; in place
of the equal sign, "therefore," "so," or "consequently"). When the
three phases of productive thinking are skillfully handled, the resulting argument, even when highly complex, will pass the test of
logic.

However, the fact that an argument is logical provides no guarantee that other people will appreciate its merit and embrace it. In fact,
if it is poorly presented, even a compelling argument has a good
chance of being rejected. This chapter explains how to present an

argument to best advantage—in other words, how to make it *persuasive* as well as sound.

A persuasive argument is one that makes people respond favorably to a viewpoint they previously rejected or were neutral toward. (If they already accept the viewpoint, there is no challenge, hence no possibility of persuasion.) The more the audience opposes the idea, the greater the challenge. The greatest mistake that any writer or speaker can make—unfortunately, a very common one—is to assume that others will be so overcome with enthusiasm for his or her ideas that they will gladly abandon their own views, even if they have held them with conviction for many years.

All that is necessary to recognize the foolishness and futility of this attitude is to consider how you react when someone expresses a view with which you disagree. Undoubtedly, your first reaction is defensive—you may feel vaguely offended and suspicious of the person's motives and begin looking for flaws in his or her idea. If you find even a slight exaggeration of a minor detail, you may be tempted to use it as an excuse for dismissing the idea completely.

Building a Persuasive Argument

The bad news is that other people will be tempted to react precisely that way to your ideas. (Even if they are too polite to express such a view, they may still think it, and silent dismissal of your argument spells failure no less than vocal denunciation does.) The good news is that by observing a few simple guidelines you can help them resist that temptation.

BEING SURE YOUR ARGUMENT IS SOUND

This is the most fundamental requirement of persuasion. Without it, persuasion is mere artifice. As noted in the previous chapter, a sound argument is one in which (a) the evidence is sufficient, (b) your assertions are true (i.e., an accurate representation of that evidence), and (c) the reasoning that leads to your judgment is free of error—specifically, illogical conclusion, hasty conclusion, oversimplification, and overgeneralization.

KNOWING YOUR AUDIENCE

You can't always know everything about an audience. Even in a small class, for example, you might know only a few of your classmates personally. Nevertheless, you can often determine the kinds of objections an audience will offer to a particular argument by their age, gender, and political, religious, or philosophic perspective. Few audiences, of course, are homogeneous in outlook, particularly if the topic is in any way controversial. Some people will be strongly pro-, others strongly con-, and many somewhere between these poles. Even people who share the same general viewpoint may have reached it by different lines of reasoning and therefore disagree about important secondary issues.

None of these complexities should daunt you. You needn't know every nuance of every person's view. It will be sufficient to understand where most people who disagree with you stand on the issue and to anticipate their reasons for disagreeing. Your best strategy is to familiarize yourself with the arguments that have been expressed in scholarly studies and in newspapers and popular magazines as well as on radio and television. Scholarly studies are likely to have influenced the views of professionals in the field and other highly educated people; popular treatments will have been more influential with the general public. Your audience's predispositions are likely to reflect the "conventional wisdom."

Consider the following three timely issues together with the speculation you could make about each without any special research. (Research would, of course, yield additional insights.)

1. *Should TV cameras be allowed in the courtroom during high-profile trials, as they were during the O. J. Simpson trial?* Those who believe

cameras should be allowed are likely to reason that the public has a right to know what transpires in the courtroom. They may also believe that public viewing of such trials will increase appreciation of the legal system and provide firsthand knowledge of the evidence, as it is presented. As a result, they would probably reason, rumors that the trial is rigged for or against the defendant would be less likely to spread, so the kind of violence that occurred following the Rodney King case would be avoided. However, those who favor *barring* cameras from the courtroom would probably reason that the cameras' presence creates a circus atmosphere, thus legitimizing and increasing the sensationalism that attends such cases and perhaps intimidating the jury and obstructing justice.

2. *Are the television and film industries responsible in any way for the plague of antisocial and criminal behavior in contemporary America?* Those who say no would undoubtedly argue that the entertainment and communication media do not cause people to behave badly (or for that matter, well); they merely hold the proverbial mirror to reality. They would tend to believe that people who try to blame the media, notably parents and teachers, are often trying to shift the blame that is properly their own. However, those who answer in the affirmative would probably reason that modern films and TV shows tend to glamorize self-indulgent and antisocial behavior and often depict adult authority figures as old-fashioned and their advice as irrelevant, thus encouraging disrespect for authority and the values on which morality and law have alike depended.

3. *Should hiring quotas based on race, ethnicity, or gender be abolished?* People who think so often have different rationales for their beliefs. Two obvious, stereotypical ones are the racist view that Caucasians are superior to other races and should enjoy preferred status in the workplace and the sexist view that males are superior to females. But many people oppose quotas because they genuinely believe that quotas represent reverse discrimination and thus are as unfair as the system they are supposed to correct. (Incidentally, to assume that someone holds a reprehensible view when it is equally possible that

he or she holds a respectable view is both illogical and unfair.) However, those who endorse hiring quotas generally believe that, whatever their imperfections, they are the fastest and best way to redress the long-standing grievances created by past injustices.

BEGINNING ON COMMON GROUND

To gain a positive first impression from people who disagree with you, begin with ideas you can be reasonably sure your audience will agree on. One way to do this is to provide background on the issue or to describe recent developments concerning it. You needn't devote a great deal of space (or in an oral presentation, time) to this—a paragraph (or a minute) will often be sufficient. An important caution: Be as objective as you can at this point, presenting only the facts and postponing any interpreting; your interpretation may be a point of contention rather than agreement. By demonstrating at the outset that you are willing to postpone judgment, you will encourage your audience to give your ideas a fair hearing.

If you were addressing the three issues discussed in the section "Know Your Audience," you might consider these possibilities, which people on either side of the issues would tend to accept. Note that although each makes a point worth expressing, readers cannot tell where the author stands on the issue. That clarification, which of course will be made later, is deliberately withheld until common ground is established.

- **On the issue of TV cameras in the courtroom:**

  In this age of communication and technological sophistication, people have become used to knowing what is happening in their neighborhoods, across the country, and around the world. Unlike their grandparents, who often learned of important events days or weeks after they happened through fourthhand reports, they are accustomed to morning, noon, and night (or in the case of CNN, *hourly*) news updates from reporters speaking live from the scene of the action.

- **On the responsibility of the media for social problems:**

  America's social problems have multiplied in recent decades. Not only are there more burglaries, rapes, assaults, and murders than before, but the character of the crimes and the attitudes of the criminals are more disturbing. Deranged people no longer shoot someone against whom they have a real or imagined grievance; they kill everyone else in that person's office or building. The victims of child molestation get younger and younger, and the perpetrators now include parents and preteenaged children. Ritual satanic murders and cannibalism, virtually unheard of half a century ago, are no longer uncommon. And more and more criminals seem to feel no regret for their deeds.

- **On the fairness of hiring quotas:**

  Anyone who ever lost out on a job to someone considerably less qualified knows how wounding the experience can be, particularly if the individual invested considerable time, effort, and money in becoming qualified. The anger provoked by a single such instance of injustice can linger for months and years. If the injustice is repeated again and again, the anger may lead to lasting resentment. If it is experienced not just by one individual but by an entire class of people—a race, religion, gender, or an ethnic group—the negative emotion generated is immeasurable. And so, however wise or foolish the device of hiring quotas may prove to have been, one thing can be said with certainty: The situation to which they were offered as a response could not have been ignored.

CLARIFYING AND SUPPORTING YOUR JUDGMENT

Invest some time and refine the statement of your conclusion about the issue. Don't settle for the first phrasing that occurs to you; experiment with different wording and choose phrasing that is precise and unambiguous. Nothing about this statement should be vague, confusing, or open to more than one interpretation. If your position is not entirely on the pro- or the anti- side of the issue but instead is a combination of the two, make clear where you agree and disagree with each side. Remember that exaggeration will give those who disagree with you an excuse to dismiss your ideas. Avoid using or implying "always" when it is more appropriate to say "usually," "sometimes," or to specify certain situations. Similarly, avoid careless use of "never" in place of "seldom," "sometimes," or specified situations and "all those people" in place of "most," "many," or specified ones.

So much for the statement of your judgment, the **what** of your argument. Even in a complex argument, this statement together with the necessary explanation seldom requires more than a paragraph or two (or a couple of minutes of an oral presentation). The rest of your presentation, the part that determines whether it will be persuasive, is the **why** of your argument, the evidence that supports your judgment and the reasoning that demonstrates that support:

- If your evidence is **anecdotal** (examples from case literature, news accounts, or personal experience), present those anecdotes in appropriate detail and demonstrate that they constitute a representative sampling rather than isolated, atypical examples.
- If your evidence is **experimental** (controlled laboratory studies), provide all essential information about the studies and explain whether they have been replicated. Keep in mind that if other researchers have been unable to verify a study's conclusions, its validity may be questionable.
- If your evidence is **statistical** (random sampling of a target group or "population"), discuss the reputation of the polling organization, the currency, size, and representativeness of the sample, and the objectivity (freedom from bias) of the questions used in the poll. In all these matters, your aim is to provide assurance that the statistics are to be trusted.
- If your evidence is **testimonial** (the expressed views of authorities), demonstrate that the authorities have expertise in the specific matter in question and indicate whether the views expressed represent a minority or a majority view in the larger community of authorities. Also, if any of the testimony was compensated, monetarily or otherwise, make that fact clear. (Being paid for testimony does not necessarily undermine the integrity of what is said, but it has been known to compromise candor.)

If any of the evidence in any of the above categories is open to more than one interpretation, demonstrate why you rejected competing interpretations and why you regard the one you chose as superior.

DEMONSTRATING FAIRMINDEDNESS

Often in controversial issues, although one side is essentially right and the other essentially wrong, neither side possesses the total truth. Fairmindedness does not mean believing that each side must be precisely half correct, which is at best a highly improbable eventuality. It means, instead, making a balanced assessment, acknowledging the valid points on each side of the dispute, however many or few such points there happen to be, and doing so graciously and generously. Because intelligent people know how difficult it is to set aside preconceived notions and to resist the urge to dismiss opposing arguments in their entirety, any effort you make to practice self-control and integrity will win you the respect of your audience and invite them to respond in kind.

AVOIDING IRRATIONAL APPEALS

Irrational appeals may fool the gullible, but when used with informed, intelligent people they are counterproductive because they suggest that the author or speaker is either ignorant or dishonest or both. The most common irrational appeals are corruptions of reasonable appeals. You may identify them as follows:

- An appeal to *emotion* is reasonable when it accompanies thought and analysis and is irrational when it substitutes for them.
- An appeal to *tradition* is reasonable when it demonstrates that the tradition still makes sense and is irrational when it argues "Let's honor it merely because it is a tradition."

- An appeal to *moderation* is reasonable when the moderate approach is the best one and is irrational when moderation is used to avoid the responsibility of judging.
- An appeal to *authority* is reasonable when it acknowledges that experts can be mistaken and is irrational when it says, in effect, "The authority has spoken, so the matter is settled."

OBSERVING THE PRINCIPLES OF EFFECTIVE EXPRESSION

It is illogical to reject an argument because it was not presented well, but that fact affords scant consolation to the writer or speaker. As was noted earlier, people who are reacting defensively will often seize on any excuse to dismiss an argument that challenges their belief. Your wisest approach is to craft all expressions of your ideas with care, whether they are formal essays or informal oral presentations in class. To be more specific,

- Arrange your ideas so as to spare your readers (listeners) confusion; use transitional words or phrases to help them see the relationship between what precedes and what follows.
- Be exact and economical in your wording, saying what you mean in as few words as possible consistent with clarity.
- Make your expression lively by avoiding clichés and by varying your sentence length, style, and structure.
- In writing, vary your paragraph length from 5 to 15 lines, aiming for an average of about 10 lines. Also, break paragraphs at appropriate places—for example, when you have finished one important point and are about to begin another.
- In speaking, enunciate clearly, speak loud enough to be heard, and maintain eye contact with your audience. If you must look down at your notes, do so as infrequently as possible, and return your gaze to your audience promptly.
- Use standard punctuation and correct spelling, grammar, and usage for all written presentations.

These standards are virtually impossible to achieve without one or more revisions of written work and review and/or rehearsal of oral presentations. Many amateur writers and speakers have difficulty accepting what every professional knows from experience—writing and formal speaking are hard work and ideas don't flow effortlessly for anyone. Strange as it may sound, professional communicators differ from amateurs mainly in their greater willingness to polish their ideas and expression. Many amateurs regard their rough drafts as finished work, whereas professionals are not satisfied until they have achieved excellence, even if that means they must do five or more drafts.

INQUIRIES

1. Select one of the issues you analyzed in Chapter 5. Write a persuasive paper of at least 500 words, following the guidelines presented in this chapter.

2. Select one of the issues you analyzed in Chapter 6. Write a persuasive paper of at least 500 words, following the guidelines presented in this chapter.

3. Select from your journal an issue you have not previously analyzed. Conduct an analysis, applying the approaches detailed in earlier chapters. Then write a persuasive paper of at least 500 words, following the guidelines presented in this chapter.

8

❧

Discussing
Sociological Issues

The scene is backstage at a television talk show. The director is giving today's guests a briefing prior to the show:

> I know you've all had a thorough introduction to the way the show operates, so I'll just quickly review what's expected of you. The key thing is to remember that the audience wants excitement and our job is to give it to them.
>
> Each of you was selected for this show because you are loud, obnoxious, and rude. We want these qualities to show through. It may help to think of the stage as a jungle and yourself and the other guests as vicious animals eager to savage one another. Whenever you see an opening to pounce on one another, go for it. I'm talking verbal pouncing, of course. We generally discourage physical attacks, unless of course the audience's attention starts to slip. In that case, . . . well, we'll cue you.

Occasionally, a guest will make the mistake of trying to understand the other person's point of view. When that happens, the show gets logical, coherent, and meaningful. That's not what we're looking for. Chaos plus confrontation equals ratings! That's our equation and, as they say in the commercial, "It works for us."

When someone says anything you disagree with, no matter how inconsequential, challenge that person. And don't wait until the person is finished speaking. Point your finger in the person's face and interrupt. It's livelier that way. If someone else interrupts the speaker before you do, interrupt that person. And always raise your voice louder than that of the person you're interrupting. In the talk show game, upping the decibel level is equivalent to trumping in card games.

One final point, our surveys show that the audience wants reality—street talk. If you talk like a charm school graduate or a college professor, they'll surf away from our program. So clip the endings off your words and use a Marlon Brando mumble. Repeat a meaningless phrase over and over until everyone who ever got past sixth grade is writhing in pain. I recommend "you know," "I mean," "you understand what I'm sayin'?" and "you get my meanin'?" Also those indispensable all-purpose words "like" and "man." And sprinkle in some obscenities.

Here's how to put it all together. Instead of saying, "I disagree with Henry's idea that civility is declining," say "You know, man, like all this stuff about civility sucks, you get my meanin'? I mean, like, I don't hafta sit here and lissen to that *@#!!. You understand what I'm sayin'?"

Remember, an aggravated audience is a happy audience. Now let's get out there and give 'em hell.

It would strain belief to suggest that any talk show director would actually instruct guests in this manner, yet readers familiar with the various talk shows on television will realize that, instructed or not, guests often *do* behave this way, and their behavior is tolerated, if not encouraged, by many hosts and directors. Accordingly, offensive behavior has become more widely accepted and practiced, creating considerable confusion about the purpose of discussion and the context necessary for that purpose to be realized.

Making Discussions Productive

The kind of discussion with which this chapter is concerned may be defined as the thoughtful exchange of ideas about serious issues by knowledgeable people for the purpose of increasing understanding and achieving insight. In many ways, this kind of discussion is more challenging than reading or writing, which are generally more tightly organized and more sharply focused. To meet that challenge, each participant must meet a high standard of cooperation and civility. The following guidelines will help you achieve this standard.

PREPARING FOR DISCUSSIONS

If the discussion is scheduled in advance, as many class discussions are, spend some time planning for it. Study the lesson or assigned issue, considering each point to be discussed. Apply your creative and critical thinking to work out your ideas and prepare to share them with others. Try to anticipate the range of views that might be expressed by others and the questions they might ask about your ideas.

BEING OPEN TO DISAGREEMENT
AND INSIGHT

When people of different backgrounds and perspectives discuss issues, disputes inevitably arise. These can be beneficial if approached constructively. The key to doing so is to detach your ego from your ideas. Even though you have given careful thought to your ideas, regard them as tentative and the discussion as an opportunity to modify and improve them. Expect others to disagree with you and criticize your view; refuse to take such criticism personally. If it develops that you have a personality clash with someone in the class, don't allow that fact to affect the class atmosphere. Make a special effort to be gracious to that person and if your generosity of spirit is not reciprocated, remember the French phrase *noblesse oblige*, the literal meaning of which is "nobility obligates." In practical terms, this means that you expect more of yourself than of others because you want to meet a higher standard of character.

No matter how intelligent you may be or how carefully you analyze an issue, you can always gain insights from others—but only if you permit yourself to do so. If you enter a discussion with the attitude that you already possess the valuable insights and no one has anything to add, you make it impossible for yourself to leave the discussion more enlightened than you entered it. This will occur only if you are open to insight and let other people's ideas stimulate your thinking. That means suspending disbelief and being willing to entertain the possibility—just the *possibility* and only for a moment—that a challenge to your idea may be valid. The key to achieving this useful attitude is to realize that you don't have to counter every idea that differs from yours. In fact, unless such ideas are offered in direct challenge in the form of a question to you, you don't have to say anything. Whenever you do decide to respond, remember that there are alternatives to getting angry and shouting down the opposition, as the following examples illustrate:

> You: The typical reaction to a new clothing or hair style is mindless acceptance. The designers pull the strings and most of us dance like puppets.
>
> A classmate: That's not the case at all. Most people give a lot of thought to the way they dress or do their hair. They don't change fashions just because some designer says so. Besides, the designers offer styles people have expressed interest in.

Standard Defensive Reaction

> You: Well, it's MY OPINION that people accept fashions mindlessly.
> The same classmate: But don't you agree that. . . .

You: (interrupting and raising your voice): NO, I DON'T AGREE. I SAID I THINK WE DANCE TO THE DESIGNERS' TUNES AND THAT'S WHAT I MEANT.

An Alternative: Modifying Your Statement

You: Maybe my puppet analogy is overstated. Still, I think people tend to accept what is fashionable without a great deal of thought. And every time they do this, they encourage designers to manipulate them in the future.

Comment: This modification is consistent with your original idea, but it presents the idea more moderately, and the fact that you are willing to do this demonstrates your desire to be reasonable and your willingness to engage in genuine dialogue, as opposed to serial monologue.

Another Alternative: Asking a Relevant Question

You: Do you mean that designers survey the public to determine what they want before creating new fashions?

Comment: Now you've shifted attention from your idea to your classmate's idea. In some cases, that might be evasive, but in this case it's not because your classmate'e notion of designers' prior consultation with the public is part of the reason for disagreeing with you. Discussion of the idea will provide you an opportunity to expose it as, at best, an oversimplification and perhaps lead your classmate a little closer to your view.

LISTENING TO OTHERS

Listening is a skill not many people have developed. Research suggests that the average person achieves only 25% to 50% efficiency listening. One reason is that when the spoken word passes the ear, it is gone. We can't look back and rehear what the other person said the way we can reread a written passage. Another reason is that listening poses a number of distractions that don't occur in reading: the speaker's facial expressions, tone of voice, physical appearance, clothing, gestures, and mannerisms. In dialogue, these distractions are multiplied by the number of people involved.

Poor listening is not merely a breach of good manners, it is also a serious obstacle to excellence in *thinking* because it prevents you from achieving the understanding that is essential to judgment. If you don't maintain attention, you'll end up disagreeing with something the other person *didn't* say, and others may attribute your blunder to lack of intelligence rather than to inattention.

To improve your listening skill, anticipate distractions, including those created by your own thought processes, and resist them when they come. For example, if another person expresses a thought that reminds you of something else, you may be tempted to stop listening and begin thinking about that. Minutes or more can pass before you drag your thoughts back to where they belong. Similarly, the habit of using the time when others are speaking to plan what you are going to say next can keep you from paying attention to them. Expect such distractions to occur, and the moment they do, exert self-discipline. Say "NOT NOW" and focus your attention on the discussion. Maintaining eye contact with the speaker is also helpful. (Lapses in attention are more likely to occur when you are looking elsewhere.)

IDENTIFYING EACH PERSON'S VIEWPOINT

Are all participants in the discussion agreeing? If so, what is the idea they share and what reasons does each person offer in support of it? If they are disagreeing, where do their views differ? What arguments does each advance for his or her view? These are important questions to have in mind as you listen. Don't try to remember every detail—just note the main point that each person makes.

Whenever possible, postpone analyzing what the other participants in the discussion say until later. Very skilled listeners can simultaneously listen and evaluate, but most people have difficulty doing so. When they start analyzing, they stop listening and miss what is said next. If ideas pop into your mind while you're listening, just jot a key word or two on paper to promote recall. But don't *ponder* them or the speakers' ideas until later.

BEING AWARE OF "GROUPTHINK"

Research by Irving Janis (1982) reveals that members of professional groups are often tempted to think alike and to stifle any inclination to disagree with the group. Such "groupthink," Janis alleges, led to President Roosevelt's failure to prepare for the Japanese attack on Pearl Harbor, President Truman's decision to invade North Korea, President Kennedy's attempt to overthrow Fidel Castro, and President Johnson's decision to escalate the Vietnam War. Among the specific defects in decision making that Janis identified are (a) consideration of a narrow rather than a broad range of possible responses to the problem or issue, (b) failure to address drawbacks to their preferred responses, even when the individuals were aware of those drawbacks, (c) failure to seek expert advice outside the group, and (d) failure to test their thinking for weaknesses or errors. Be sure these defects do not compromise your discussions.

ACKNOWLEDGING COMPLEXITY

Many of the statements made and positions taken in discussion are partly valid and partly invalid. Don't have the attitude that your only options are to agree completely or to disagree completely. More often than not, the most reasonable response to someone else's idea will be to agree in part and disagree in part.

RAISING PROBING QUESTIONS

The following questions, which are similar to those posed in Chapter 7, have broad application. The subject of the specific discussion and the ideas expressed may, of course, suggest additional questions.

Does any one of the speakers have a special bias? If so, does that person seem to make an effort to control it and be fairminded? Bias is a tendency to favor one view over another. Because past experience shapes our thinking, bias is often unavoidable. It becomes a fault only when we surrender our judgment to it. You may not always be able to detect a speaker's bias, but you can identify fairmindedness by noting whether that person refrains from distorting opposing views and offers reasons for accepting some ideas and rejecting others. (Remember that taking a forceful position is not necessarily a sign of bias or unfairness.)

Has any one of the speakers excluded any important evidence? If so, does that evidence support or challenge the speaker's position? Omissions of evidence can easily occur in discussion, quite unintentionally. The speaker may be aware of only part of the evidence and form his or her judgment accordingly. Or the speaker may be familiar with all the evidence but forget to refer to part of it. Because conversation is more spontaneous than writing, forgetting is more common. You may have to consult one or more experts or at least do additional reading before you can decide whether all important evidence has been presented. Be sure to consider your own experience and observation, too. Even if you have no formal expertise in the matter, you may have encountered other situations that are relevant. To lack respect for the expertise of professional sociologists is presumptuous, but it is no sign of disrespect to incorporate your experience into your assessments—learning to do so, in fact, is the only way to learn how to think like a sociologist.

What other interpretations of the evidence are possible? Even experts may disagree over what the evidence means and what implications it has for the issue being discussed. For decades, research on public assistance programs has documented that some families remain on welfare generation after generation. Some authorities regard this evidence as proof that public assistance programs make people lazy. But others reject this interpretation, arguing that social conditions and lack of educational opportunity prevent many people from becoming self-sufficient. Never assume that the first interpretation you hear is the most reasonable one; search out other interpretations and make careful comparisons.

Has any speaker misstated facts or committed errors in reasoning? Both errors of fact and errors in reasoning are common in discussion, especially if the exchange of ideas is spirited. So be alert for misstatements of fact and errors of judgment, and more specifically, for hasty conclusions, overgeneralizations, oversimplifications, and unwarranted assumptions. Here's how to do so: Ask if each speaker's evidence provides adequate support for his or her assertion; determine if any speaker has labeled an entire group on the basis of a few isolated experiences with individuals or has distorted a complex reality; and decide whether, in analyzing the issue, any speaker has taken too much for granted.

DECIDING WHICH VIEW
IS MOST REASONABLE

Answer the questions you raise about the discussion and, on that basis, decide where wisdom lies. Don't assume that one person must be entirely right and the others entirely wrong. Frequently, each will be partly right and partly wrong. Thus, the most reasonable view may not have been expressed at all—you may have to construct it by combining the various insights of the speakers into a new view.

In making your decision, remember that the speaker who dominates a discussion is not necessarily right, even if he or she persuades the other people. Forcefulness and eloquence are not synonymous with soundness. Be sure to judge fairly instead of merely repeating what you have always thought and dismissing other ideas. It is a mark of a good thinker to recognize and accept other people's insights, especially when they challenge your own. If you lack sufficient information to judge an important point, withhold judgment until you have obtained that information.

BEING COOPERATIVE AND COURTEOUS

Keep in mind that time limitations may exist and the discussion leader, whether a professor or a fellow student, will have the difficult task of keeping discussion moving and ensuring that all individuals have a chance to speak and all perspectives are heard. Be sympathetic and understand if you don't get all the time you'd like. Also, remember the rules of civility, especially at those moments when you are tempted to violate them—that is, whenever views clash and discussion grows heated. Refrain from interrupting (even if others do), raising your voice, and exhibiting other displays of incivility. Try your best to give no offense yourself and resist the urge to take offense at others.

MONITORING YOUR CONTRIBUTIONS

People who exercise no restraint in speaking, who feel compelled to offer a lengthy commentary on every point of discussion, seemingly unaware that others might have something to say, are seldom esteemed by their associates. And those who bring to every discussion a spirit of contentiousness, ever ready to nitpick other people's ideas, call to mind the saying that some people brighten a room by leaving it. Does this mean you shouldn't express your ideas freely? That you should refrain from disagreeing with fellow students, textbook authors, and professors? Not at all. It means only that excellence in discussion requires proportion and a sense of timing, and you will be a better and more accepted contributor to discussion if you give careful thought to when you should speak and when you should remain silent.

Analyze your contributions to group discussions. If you find yourself dominating, speak a little less often or more briefly. One good way to do this is to limit your contributions to matters you regard as most important—using one example instead of the four you could mention, offering two reasons instead of the six you have in mind. Conversely, if you tend to let others do all the talking, make an effort to speak more frequently. If others seem to express your ideas before you have had a chance to, try this tactic—whenever "your" idea has already been expressed, state your agreement with it and add your personal reasons for thinking as you do. They are likely to be different from other people's reasons.

INQUIRY

Note: To facilitate discussion, all students should conduct the same inquiry. (The choice of that inquiry may, of course, be democratically decided.)

1. Analyze one of the following topics, applying the approaches you learned in this book. Prepare for a class discussion by reviewing the guidelines presented in this chapter.

   ■ Do the news media focus too much on the sensational or the negative? Do they present a false picture of what life in this country is really like for most people? If so, what effect does this have on people's habits and attitudes?

   ■ To what extent and in what ways do instructors at your college encourage independence of mind in students?

   ■ Television is a passive activity; viewers watch other people doing something but have no opportunity to become involved in what is done. Does this passivity cause any problems, such as a loss of initiative or a reluctance to take a stand on important issues?

Contemporary Issues
in Sociology

The following list is a modest sampling of the issues of concern to sociologists. The reading you do for your course and reflection on your experiences and observations will suggest many other issues.

- Does the fact that young children are imitative make the impact of television greater on them than on adults? Do commercials in Saturday cartoons take unfair advantage of children? If so, how?

- Do violent movies and television shows brutalize people, making them insensitive to other people's suffering? Do such shows increase the tendency to be violent? Do they create such a tendency where it didn't previously exist? Are the effects of media violence greater on children than on adults?

- To what extent were children's attitudes and values shaped by each of the following agencies 50 years ago: (a) the home, (b) the school, (c) the church, and (d) the entertainment and communications media? To what extent has the situation changed today?

- What effect, if any, do magazines devoted to gossip about entertainers have on the ideas and aspirations of those who read them?

- Do the lyrics of heavy metal and rap music create antisocial attitudes in those who listen to that music regularly? Is there any connection between such music and antisocial behavior?

- What effect, if any, does advertising have on people's habits and values? Do the themes of advertising create any harmful attitudes?

- Is there any connection between the messages of mass culture and social problems? For example, do appeals to self-indulgence and instant gratification lead to substance abuse? To teenage pregnancy? To violence? To theft?

- Does mass culture tend to decrease students' respect for parents and teachers? Does it cause students to lose their motivation to learn? Is it responsible for the deficiencies in knowledge and skills reported in recent years?

- Who should be held accountable for the negative effects of mass culture? The people who run the various agencies, such as the television networks and the movie studios? The advertising agencies? The sponsors? The public? What can be done about these negative effects?

- Does crowding—for example, in inner-city housing—increase aggressiveness?

- What factors lead people to join cults?

- Does the advertising industry's and the media's promotion of slenderness as the standard of beauty have any effect on the incidence of anorexia nervosa?

- Are older people less productive in their careers than younger people? If so, at what point in life does productivity most sharply decline? Are the answers to these questions different for the various professions?

- What well-known men and women are most admired by today's preteenagers? Teenagers? Adults ages 20 to 40? Forty to 60? Over 60?

- What characteristics do inventors have in common? How do those differ from the characteristics of noninventors?

- What interesting rumors are currently circulating on your campus? How did they get started? What are the dynamics of the process by which they have been transmitted?

- What are the tenets of secular humanism? How has it developed in this century, and what influence has it had at various times? Is it a form of religion?

- Has the middle class in the United States increased, decreased, or stayed about the same size over the past century? If it has increased or decreased, what has caused the change?

- Are the attitudes of Caucasian men toward gender equality different from the attitudes of African American men? Oriental men? Hispanic men? Are there also differences among the various ethnic groups comprising Caucasian men? If there are significant differences, how are they best explained?

- What factors influence people to accept or reject a new clothing or hair style? Are the factors the same for both men and women? Are men more or less accepting of changes in clothing style than women are? Hair styles?

- What well-known men and women do students at your college most admire? What qualities do they most admire in those individuals?

- Are children who play with toy guns more or less likely than others to own guns when they are adults?

References

American Sociological Association. (1989). *Code of ethics.* Washington, DC: Author.

Anderson, H. H. (Ed.). (1959). *Creativity and its cultivation.* New York: Harper.

Arkes, H. (1994, July-August). German judges and undue burdens. *Crisis,* p. 16.

Arkes, H. R. (1991, August). *Some practical judgment/decision making research.* Paper presented at the annual meeting of the American Psychological Association, Boston.

Asch, S. E. (1952). *Social psychology.* Englewood Cliffs, NJ: Prentice Hall.

Asch, S. E. (1965). Effects of group pressure upon the modification and distortion of judgments. In H. Proshansky & B. Seidenbert (Eds.), *Basic studies in social psychology.* New York: Holt, Rinehart & Winston.

Barnard, C. I. (1938). *The functions of the executive.* Cambridge, MA: Harvard University Press.

Bibby, R., & Brinkerhoff, M. (1973). Circulation of the saints revisited: A longitudinal look at conservative church growth. *Journal for the Scientific Study of Religion, 22,* 253-262.

Chambliss, D. E. (1995). The mundanity of excellence: An ethnographic report on stratification and Olympic swimmers. In D. M. Newman (Ed.), *Sociology: Exploring the architecture of everyday life. Readings* (pp. 4-19). Thousand Oaks, CA: Pine Forge Press.

Comarow, M. (1993, December 15). Are sociologists above the law? *Chronicle of Higher Education*, p. A44.

Domhoff, G. W. (1995). The bohemian grove. In D. M. Newman (Ed.), *Sociology: Exploring the architecture of everyday life. Readings* (pp. 215-222). Thousand Oaks, CA: Pine Forge Press.

Feder, D. (1993). *A Jewish conservative looks at pagan America*. Lafayette, LA: Huntington House.

Fishman, M. (1995). Crime waves as ideology. In D. M. Newman (Ed.), *Sociology: Exploring the architecture of everyday life. Readings* (pp. 42-49). Thousand Oaks, CA: Pine Forge Press.

Frankl, V. (1978). *The unheard cry for meaning*. New York: Simon & Schuster.

Giele, J. Z. (1988). Gender and sex roles. In N. J. Smelser (Ed.), *Handbook of sociology* (pp. 291-324). Newbury Park, CA: Sage.

Gilligan, C. (1982). *In a different voice*. Cambridge, MA: Harvard University Press.

Gitlin, T. (1980). *The whole world is watching*. Berkeley: University of California Press.

Harris, E. E. (1969, Spring). Respect for persons. *Daedalus*, p. 113.

Hitchcock, J. (1982). *What is secular humanism? Why humanism became secular and how it is changing our world*. Harrison, NY: RC Books.

Hofstede, G. (1988, Summer). Motivation, leadership, and organizations: Do American theories apply abroad? *Organizational Dynamics*, pp. 42-63.

Howell, W. C., & Dipboye, R. L. (1986). *Essentials of industrial and organizational psychology*. Homewood, IL: Dorsey.

Janis, I. L. (1982). *Groupthink: Psychological studies of policy decisions* (2nd ed.). Boston: Houghton Mifflin.

Jepson, R. W. (1967). *Clear thinking*. New York: Longmans, Green.

Joy, L. A., Kimball, M. M., & Zabrack, M. L. (1988). Television and children's aggressive behavior. In R. M. Liebert & J. Sprafkin, *The early window: Effects of television on children and youth* (3rd ed.). New York: Pergamon.

Levin, J. (1993). *Sociological snapshots*. Newbury Park, CA: Pine Forge Press.

Liebert, R. M., & Sprafkin, J. (1988). *The early window: Effects of television on children and youth* (3rd ed.). New York: Pergamon.

McCormack, P. (1981, November 8). Good news for the underdog. *Santa Barbara News Press*, p. 10D.

Minerbrook, S. (1994, August 8). The forgotten pioneers. *U.S. News & World Report*, p. 53.

Piaget, J. (1991). *Plays, dreams, and imitation in childhood*. Reprinted in E. Loftus & K. Ketcam, *Witness for the defense* (pp. 17-19). New York: St. Martin's.

Reisman, J. A., & Eichel, E. W. (1990). *Kinsey, sex, and fraud*. Lafayette, LA: Huntington House.

Risman, B. J. (1987). Intimate relationships from a microstructural perspective: Men who mother. *Gender & Society, 1*(1), 6-32.

Rogers, C. R. (1961). *On becoming a person: A therapist's view of psychotherapy*. Boston: Houghton Mifflin.

Ronai, C. R. (1992). A night in the life of an erotic dancer/researcher. In C. Ellis & M. G. Flaherty (Eds.), *Investigating subjectivity: Research on lived experience* (pp. 102-124). Newbury Park, CA: Sage.

Rosenthal, R. (1973). The Pygmalion effect lives. *Psychology Today*, pp. 56-63.

Schlesinger, A. M., Jr. (1993). *The disuniting of America: Reflections on a multicultural society.* New York: W. W. Norton.

See, K. O., & Wilson, W. J. (1988). Race and ethnicity. In N. J. Smelser (Ed.), *Handbook of sociology* (pp. 223-242). Newbury Park, CA: Sage.

Sherman, B. R., & Kunda, Z. (1989, August). *Motivated evaluation of scientific evidence.* Paper presented at the annual meeting of the American Psychological Society, Arlington, VA.

Sorokin, P. A. (1927). *Social and cultural mobility.* New York: Harper.

Szasz, T. (1990). *Insanity: The idea and its consequences.* New York: John Wiley.

Tavris, C. (1989). *Anger: The misunderstood emotion.* New York: Simon & Schuster.

Tavris, C. (1992). *The mismeasure of woman.* New York: Simon & Schuster.

Tuchman, G. (1988). Mass media institutions. In N. J. Smelser (Ed.), *Handbook of sociology* (pp. 601-626). Newbury Park, CA: Sage.

Vitz, P. C. (1994). *Psychology as religion: The cult of self-worship* (2nd ed.). Grand Rapids, MI: Eerdmans.

Wade, C. (1993, November-December). A psychological perspective on critical thinking. *Inquiry: Critical Thinking Across the Disciplines*, pp. 15-19.

Weisman, J. (1991, March 6). Though still a target of attacks, self-esteem movement advances. *Education Week*, p. 1.

Index

About the Author

Vincent Ryan Ruggiero is Professor Emeritus at the State University of New York at Delhi where he taught courses in the humanities for 28 years, simultaneously serving as department chair for 13 years, retiring in 1989. While at SUNY, Delhi he designed courses in creative and critical thinking and developed teaching materials, most of which became textbooks. Since then, he has devoted his time to writing, speaking, and consulting both in the United States and abroad on such topics as ethics, communication, educational reform, and organizational efficiency.

Considered a pioneer in the teaching of thinking, he has delivered featured presentations at national and international conferences and conducted faculty development seminars at over 60 colleges and universities. He is listed in the *Directory of American Scholars* and *Who's Who in American Education*. Three of his speeches, notably his July 1994 keynote address at the Sixth Annual International Conference on Thinking, have been published in *Vital Speeches of the Day*, a journal devoted to excellence in thought and expression.

He is author of 75 articles and 16 books on thinking and related subjects, among them *The Elements of Rhetoric, Enter the Dialogue, The Art of Thinking,* and *Warning: Nonsense Is Destroying America.* The PBS television series "Author, Author" featured him in a one-hour segment, and he has created and narrated two one-hour special presentations on education, also shown on PBS, which were sponsored by the Virginia State Education Department.

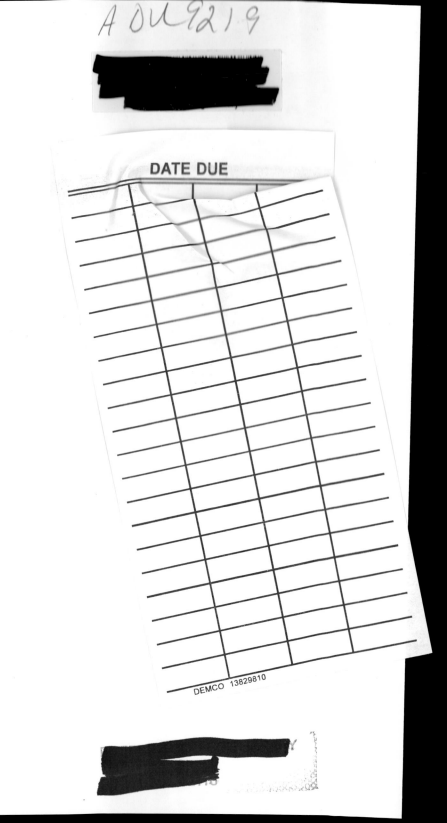

DATE DUE